I0542857

GROWING UP IN
SOUTH ARABIA

GROWING UP IN
SOUTH ARABIA

AHMAD AL SARI

Copyright © 2022 Ahmad Al Sari

All rights reserved.

Published in association with Per Capita Publishing, a division of Content Capital®.

No part of this book may be reproduced, stored in a retrieval system, or transmitted by any means, electronic, mechanical, photocopying, recording, or otherwise, without written permission from the copyright holder.

Although the author and publisher have made every effort to ensure that the information in this book was correct at press time, the author and publisher do not assume and hereby disclaim any liability to any party for any loss, damage, or disruption caused by errors or omissions, whether such errors or omissions result from negligence, accident, or any other cause.

ISBN 13: 978-1-954020-38-2 (Paperback)
ISBN 13: 978-1-954020-39-9 (Ebook)

Library of Congress Cataloging-in-Publication Data
Names: Al Sari, Ahmad, author.
Title: Growing Up in South Arabia / Ahmad Al Sari
Description: First Edition | Texas: Per Capita Publishing (2022)
Identifiers: LCCN 2022918945 (print)

First Edition

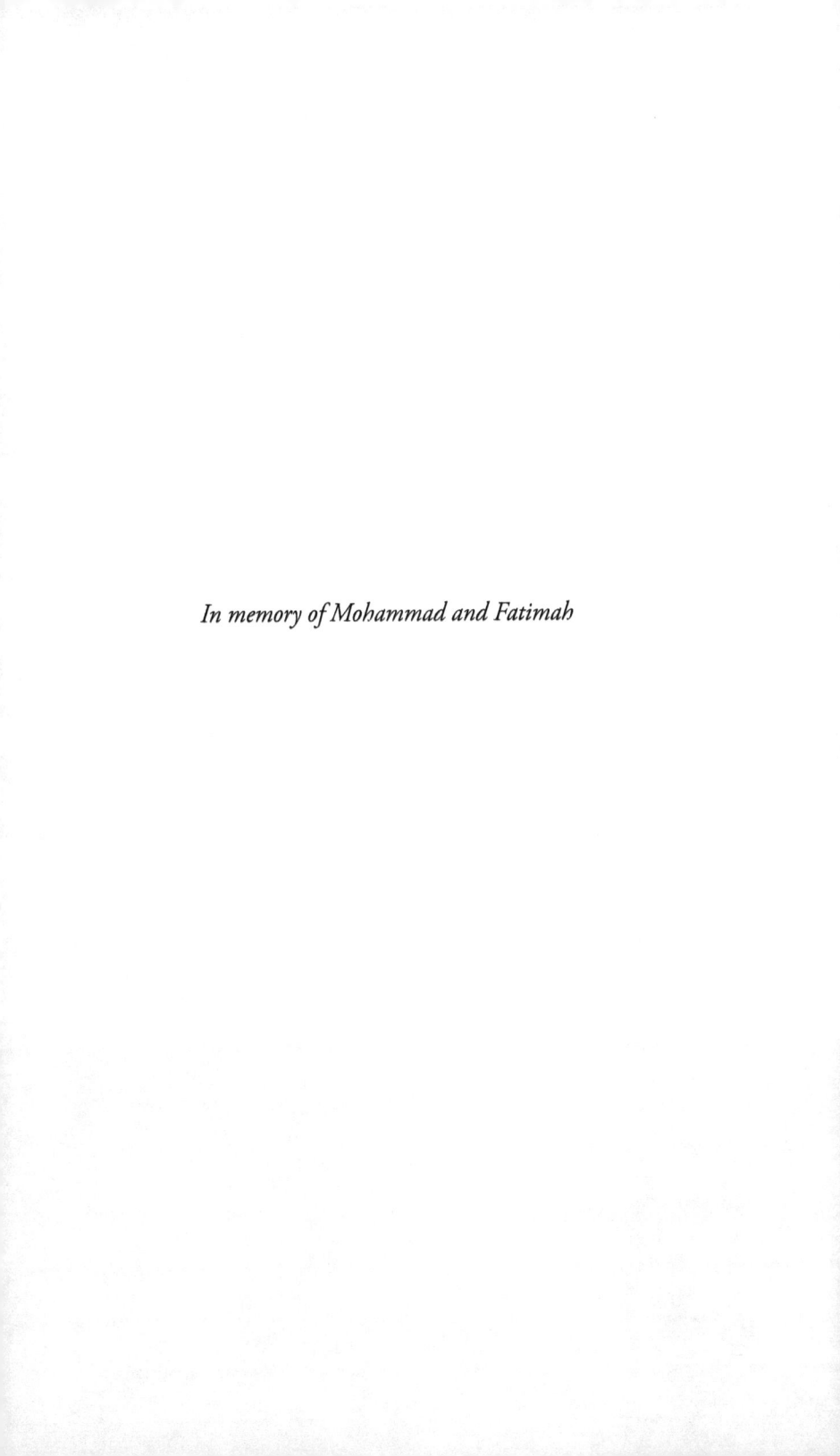

In memory of Mohammad and Fatimah

TABLE OF CONTENTS

PREFACE

I wanted to tell the world about the place where I was born and grew up before being uprooted to Saudi Arabia in 1956. I became one of millions around the world who move about with an invisible umbilical cord tying them to the old place. There seems to be a Hadhramaut gene encoded in all of us. It passes through generations to keep us all tuned to the land, its history, its deep valleys, and especially its customs and values.

I wanted to write about events within Hadhramaut and around it in the first decade after the end of World War II. The events of the time shaped the Arab World of today and caused considerable death and destruction along the way.

As a boy, this is how I perceived the things that were happening to my family, my town, my country, and my region.

1.

THE CONCORD

I gripped the arm rests of my seat as the Concorde roared down the Charles de Gaulle Airport runway and noisily lifted itself like a gigantic bird of prey. It was my first experience on the Concorde, which would leave Paris and land in Washington, DC, in less than four hours. I would have to set my watch back one hour upon landing at Dulles International Airport, as I would arrive "earlier" than I departed.

This was the year 1979, and I was traveling on business as an advisor to a scientific institution of the Government of Saudi Arabia with an executive of the institution. We had the opportunity to spend two days in Paris, staying at the Prince de Galles Hotel, and had used the few hours we had before the flight to visit the Louvre to view its priceless treasures and historical artifacts.

Soon the Concorde reached cruising altitude and the digital speed display at the front of the cabin reached Mach 2. I was not sure what would happen when the Concorde broke the sound barrier. But I felt nothing, and the plane was now rocketing at twice the speed of sound. I had not expected to ever fly on the Concorde, but my trip companion arranged it, and I was grateful to him for the experience to be on this marvel of modern air travel.

I finally relaxed as the stewardess began serving the gourmet lunch in four courses, starting with beluga caviar and ending with excellent coffee.

As I lowered the back of the narrow seat and closed my eyes, I thought of the many countries that I had visited, the many people I encountered, and the experiences I had around the world. But my mind finally wandered back to Al Mukalla, the little town on the Arabian Sea where I was born. I remembered standing on the beach gazing at the ocean as a school of dolphins moved in formation and jumped in and out of the water, looking like a giant dragon. People of Al Mukalla said it was a dragon searching for King Solomon's ring. In the distance, there were two ships waiting to unload their cargo, then nothing but a shimmering blue ocean and an infinite horizon. My ears filled with the roar of the Indian Ocean as the waves broke on the rocky beach.

Snapping back from my reverie, I realized that the roar in my ears was that of the Concorde's engines and not the Indian Ocean.

I felt gratified to have realized most of my childhood dreams of seeing every continent on Earth and coming in touch with their peoples and cultures. I felt that I owed much to Al Mukalla, and I decided to write a book about it one day.

2.

UPRISING AND DEATH

It was a day like any other in 1952 in Al Mukalla. After breakfast, Father walked his customary path to his office, which was near the port in the Eastern part of Al Mukalla. Our nanny, Sehala, had gone off to her family home the week before, having been upset by something or another, and Father managed to get a 13-year-old boy, Saleh, to come help with the cleaning and shopping. His family had recently moved to Al Mukalla from the interior of the country and needed some income.

Saleh was sweeping the floors around 10:00 that morning when he noticed groups of men moving in the street below, heading down the street toward the sea before turning and heading to the Sultan's palace. As he watched, he saw the number of men moving toward the palace grow in number, which made him increasingly curious. He went down to the street, asked the men a few questions, and returned to tell Mother that the men were heading to the palace to protest.

She did not know much about the politics of the day, and we children were even more oblivious, but she could sense the agitation in the air, a possible danger coming. Despite the growing tension, things were quiet for the next few hours and by noon, Mother put us in bed for our mid-day nap. Unbeknownst to us, as we sank into deep slumber, soldiers were spreading across the top of the mountain overlooking the town. Curious, Saleh wanted to go down to observe the street, but Mother managed to stop him, so he ran up to the roof. He then reported to Mother that armed soldiers had taken positions on the mountain top, and her apprehension turned into fear, then pure panic as she heard the faint sound of shots firing.

I was five years old, blissfully enjoying my nap—that is, until I was shaken awake by my very disturbed mother. No more dreaming and cozy covers. I was yanked out of bed, and Mother herded me, my younger brother, and my sister along the corridor into her bedroom and hid us under her large bed. Her raw panic infected us all, and we began to cry.

Time both slowed down and sped up; it is hard to tell how long this lasted before Father showed up and brought us out from under the bed. He did his best to calm us down.

He then led me to the window overlooking the hospital yard and left me there. I was too young to contemplate Father's reasoning for placing me in the window to see the tragic view below; but as I thought about it later in life, I concluded that he thought fear of the unknown is worse for a child than seeing the painful truth.

Trucks were coming in, full of injured or unmoving people. I noticed Uncle Hussain—my mother's uncle—standing on one truck and helping unload the dead and wounded to be taken inside the hospital. By then, the town was calm, and peace was restored. I was too shocked to feel any emotion. It was like watching a movie; I felt a complete detachment, my nerves shot after the hours of stress and hiding. The scene was etched in my memory forever, and it was not until much later that I realized this experience influenced the way I react to stressful situations.

On a positive note, Curious Saleh survived his time on the roof unscathed, even as the bullets streamed down from the top of the mountain.

In the following days, as we were repairing the damage done to our town and our hearts, I heard Father try to explain to Mother why it had happened in the first place. The crisis started with the retirement of Shaikh Saif, the highly respected Secretary of State of Al Qu'aiti Sultanate, at the end of his term in office in 1952. He was from Oman, whereas the Education Supervisor (Minister) who vied for the Secretary of State position and was vouched for by the British Resident Advisor, was from the Sudan. A local political group objected vehemently to the appointment of yet another foreigner and pushed for the appointment of a local. One candidate was the assistant to the retiring Secretary of State, who happened to be my maternal uncle, Abdulrahman.

A group of citizens had shown their displeasure by protesting outside the Sultan's palace that morning but were kept at a distance by the armed Sultani guards. The crowd steadily grew, emotions flared, and one of the demonstrators grabbed the gun of one of the guards, which encouraged the rest of the crowd to push forward. In the melee, shots were fired and some of the demonstrators were killed. This prompted the commander of the Sultani guards to advise the Sultan to keep the peace by utilizing the regular army. The troops, many of whom knew or were related to the protestors, were summoned and surrounded the palace. Many empathized with the gripes of the demonstrators, so while keeping them away from the palace entrance, they did not interfere with the demonstration.

However, the British Resident Advisor, successor to longtime diplomat Harold Ingrams, advised the Sultan to declare a curfew and nip the demonstration in the bud before it spread by calling in the Badiah army, which was based in a suburb called Addees. This army consisted of Bedouins who paid blind allegiance to the Sultan and were under British command.

The demonstrators learned of the Badiah army's involvement, and some ran to the town gate, overpowered the guards, and closed the gate, thus sealing the town from the west. In response, Badiah army snipers ascended the mountain from the west and took positions at the top of the mountain overlooking the town, while others descended and attacked along the main road. Demonstrators defying or not understanding orders to clear the streets faced violent opposition, including one who lay dead in the street outside our home. With the announcement of a curfew and learning of the approaching Badiah army, many of the demonstrators had dispersed and gone home. The diehards who continued to demonstrate either ran away later from the Badiah Army or were shot.

Thus, the will of the British Resident Advisor prevailed, and the Sudanese Education Supervisor was sworn in as Secretary of State. My uncle Abdulrahman, whose leadership opportunity had been thwarted, decided to leave the country, crossing the border into Saudi Arabia. As with all tragedy, life soon went back to the way it was. The violent crisis had lasted one day, followed by days of mourning the dead and tending to the injured.

The civil leaders who resisted the appointment of the new Secretary of State chose not to pursue the matter, and some of them immigrated to other countries. Hadhramis are generally a pacifist people who rarely resort to violent means to resist or affect change. They also knew that the Sultan had long ceded sovereignty to the British, whose power was unparalleled in the area at that time.

3.

AL MUKALLA, HADHRAMAUT

Al Mukalla was the capital of Al Qu'aiti Sultanate on the southern coast of the Arabian Peninsula. The territory stretches nearly 1,000 kilometers, from the border of Oman to Yemen, and was then called South Arabia. The largest area within South Arabia was Hadhramaut. It hosted four states, the largest of which was Al Qu'aiti Sultanate. Each state was named after its ruling family or tribe. Thus, the Al Qu'aiti family ruled Al Qu'aiti Sultanate, Al Kathiri Sultanate was under the rule of the Al Kathiri family, the Abdulwahid family governed Al Wahidi Sultanate, and Al Mahra Sultanate was named after the ancient tribe that inhabited the area.

Al Mukalla was a natural harbour on the Arabian Sea and the capital of Al Qu'aiti Sultanate. It had replaced Alshihr, which lay 40 kilometers northeast, as the main port and seat of government in the mid-nineteenth century. The town sat on a kilometer-wide strip of land between the sea and the mountain on its northern border. The terrain to the east was an area called Khalf (meaning "rear"), made difficult to traverse by many large boulders; this made the narrow road in and out of Al Mukalla easily defensible. The west side was sealed by a wall stretching from mountain to sea, with a single large gate allowing controlled access, and the mountain was lined with a string of small stone buildings called *koots* that housed artillery guns to defend against attacking ships. The town was essentially a natural fortress.

Al Mukalla and neighbouring Alshihr were major ports ruled by different, feuding rulers in the nineteenth century. Both ports were used to import slaves from Africa until 1863, when the rulers of both towns signed friendship treaties with the British Crown. Given Britain's presence as a colonial power in Aden, the regional rulers were eager to be friends with Big Brother. The treaties included pledges to halt the import or export of slaves, but they did not yet include a provision for protection. This allowed Al Qu'aitis to use their wealth and resources acquired in Hyderabad to overcome Al Kasadis, who ruled Al Shihr, and bring most of the coast under their control. In 1873 they signed a protection treaty with the British Crown that codified the banning of slavery and the slave trade. This treaty also gave Britain all power regarding external relations, but left all internal affairs solely in the hands of the ruler (the Sultan).

All slaves were freed and joined public life as equal citizens. They integrated with the rest of society, with some gaining social status as members of the regular army. They rose in rank to become commanders of army units. Under the Al Qu'aiti Sultanate, they even became governors of towns like Shibam and Al Mukalla.

In early March 1947, the ruler was Sultan Saleh bin Ghalib Al Qu'aiti, who had succeeded his uncle, Omar bin Awadh Al Qu'aiti, in 1936. His succession to his uncle was based on the recorded will of his grandfather, which alternated succession between his two sons, Ghalib and Omar, and their descendants, thereafter. Ghalib, being the elder of the two brothers, succeeded his father Awadh. He was then succeeded by his younger brother, Omar. The Sultanate then reverted to Omar's nephew, Saleh, who would then be succeeded by the son of Omar.

Sultan Saleh was a popular and educated ruler who sought to advance and reform society. He was conscious of many challenges he faced, including primitive infrastructure, low literacy rates, weak or non-existent health services, undeveloped systems of government, and the constant warring among various tribes. In agreeing to cede considerable control to the British Crown as part of the protection treaty, he hoped to obtain expertise and resources to move the country forward. One significant accomplishment that has not received sufficient recognition was his ability to codify the penal code based on Islamic Shariah, whereby offenses were defined and respective penalties outlined; thus streamlining the legal system and giving judges clear and helpful guidelines to follow.

4.

THE INGRAMS

The British had arrived in Aden, about 500 kilometers to the west of Al Mukalla, in 1839, and claimed it as a British colony before extending their influence over the whole of South Arabia. Aden was a natural harbour near Bab Al Mandab, the strait connecting the Red Sea to the Indian Ocean, and served as a perfect station between Europe and India. After the opening of the Suez Canal in 1869, it became a port of call for all ships sailing to and from Europe.

Harold and Doreen Ingrams were the only English names many children heard in the 1930s and '40s in Hadhramaut; Harold Ingrams had arrived in Aden as a political officer in 1934 and was assigned the task of overseeing the Eastern Protectorates, which was mainly the Hadhramaut area. The Ingramses were discussed often because they blended with Hadhramis of all social strata. Harold and Doreen often toured Hadhramaut on the backs of camels and donkeys, eventually producing a report he titled "A Report on the Political, Social and Economic Conditions of Hadhramaut." They connected and broke bread with rich and poor, and they were invited into homes with little reservation. Their command of the local dialect and habit of wearing Arab clothes lifted all barriers between them and the community. Hence, his report was a detailed and comprehensive treatise on the social, economic, and political life in Hadhramaut and established him as an expert on the country.

A couple of years after landing in Hadhramaut and releasing his report, Harold Ingrams became a close advisor to Sultan Saleh Al Qu'aiti and worked with him to reform and advance Hadhrami society. Ingrams was in support of the Sultan Saleh's son, Awadh, to succeed his father, although this contravened the recorded will of Sultan Saleh's grandfather. It must be said that Awadh was an adult, while the next in line was still a child. This helped convince Sultan Saleh to accept the amendment to the Protection Treaty to host a British Resident Advisor whose advice was to be followed in all manners except for religion and customs, on the condition that Harold Ingrams be that Advisor. Sultan Saleh was apparently confident that Ingrams was sufficiently educated in the religion and customs of the people and shared the Sultan's goals for the advancement of Hadhrami society. With the Empire's might and resources behind Ingrams, Sultan Saleh reasoned that sharing his powers with Ingrams was in the interest of the country.

This signing of the amended protection agreement in 1937 allowed British control of internal affairs. Economic development was hampered by the constant warring and feuding among tribes and clans, so Ingrams initiated air raids to quell the violence among tribes. The raids killed many civilians in the process but forced a temporary peace. He then proceeded to broker a peace accord among the tribes that required the agreement of nearly 1,400 *mogaddams* (chiefs). The agreement was for three years, later extended to 10, and came to be known as the "Ingrams Peace." Trade flourished as a result of the peace, and people felt its value and benefits. Meanwhile, his wife Doreen's command of the local dialect, knowledge of local customs, and deep empathy with women gained her entry into the hearts of local women, who hosted her in their homes and shared their problems and feelings.

Many older folks, while singing the praises of Sultan Saleh, strongly rebuke him for signing the treaty that gave the British de facto control over the internal affairs of the state. On the other hand, despite the broad powers allowed him by the Protection Treaty, Ingrams was never intent on imposing British-style democracy. He believed in helping the people of Hadhramaut work out their own problems and arrive at their own solutions. This made his role as resident advisor effective and earned him a place in the modern history of Hadhramaut.

While Harold and Doreen Ingrams empathized with the people of Hadhramaut and influenced their lives in a positive way, it must be remembered that they were agents of the British Empire, whose interests came first. The Empire desired South Arabia's strategic location, and an unruly population made it difficult to control the land. The peace that was good for the area was also good for the Empire. While there was little economic gain to the Empire from South Arabia, it did not cost much to keep it under British control. By comparison, India offered considerably more economic value and was first colonized by the East India Company. This company grew to control half the world trade in the middle of the eighteenth century, including commodities like cotton, silk, indigo, dye, salt, spices, saltpeter, tea, and opium. The East India Company ruled for a hundred years before the British government took over in the mid-nineteenth century. Economic development of India was financed only to the extent that benefited the British Empire, including a good railroad infrastructure. When the British left, India was still a poor country.

5.
EID TRADITIONS

There are two major holidays in Islam. Eid Al Fitr ("the feast of breaking the fast") falls on the first day of Shawwal, the tenth month in the Muslim lunar calendar, following the holy month of Ramadhan, when Muslims fast every day of this month. The other holiday is Eid Al Adha ("the feast of sacrifice") which falls on the tenth day of the Thul Hijja, the twelfth month of the Muslim calendar. It corresponds to the second day of the pilgrimage to Makkah (Mecca), when pilgrims sacrifice sheep or other cattle for charity. It is also a custom of many Muslims around the world to sacrifice camels, cows, sheep, or goats on the same day and distribute the meat to the poor, their neighbors, and their relatives. The two major holidays are only around 70 days apart.

Because they are based on the lunar calendar, which is eleven days shorter than the solar calendar year, they fall in the middle of summer in one year and in the middle of winter, sixteen years later.

Fasting the holy month of Ramadhan is the fourth of five pillars of Islam, which are in the following order of importance:

1. The attestation that there is no god other than the One God and that Mohammad is a messenger of God.

2. Praying five time every day.

3. Paying the annual *zakat* (a tax for the support of the poor).

4. Fasting the holy month of Ramadhan.

5. Performing the pilgrimage to Makkah once in a lifetime, if possible in means and physical ability.

The key pillar of Islam is the first, the attestation to the oneness of God and that Mohammad is God's messenger. In fact, there is a saying of the Prophet Mohammad that states, "He who declares that there is no God but the One God enters heaven."

Muslims believe in all messengers of the One God in the Jewish and Christian faith, including Ibrahim (Abraham), Moses (Mousa), Jacob (Yacoub), Joseph (Yousuf) and Jesus (Isa). They believe in the immaculate birth of Jesus from his mother, the Virgin Mary (Mariam). But they stop short of considering Jesus the son of God. Muslims believe that Mariam was impregnated with a spirit from God to bear Jesus, but that Jesus was still a creation and messenger, and not a son, of the One God who created everything in the universe. To elevate any of God's creations to his level would be heresy in Islam.

Still, Jews and Christians are considered "People of the Book" who were welcome to practice their religions in Muslim land in peace and be treated as equal citizens—such as was the case in Spain under Muslim rule—and where there is a sizeable population of both at this time, in places like Egypt or Lebanon. In fact, there is a verse in the Quran that many are ignorant of. It translates into: "Believers, Jews, Christians, and Sabieen (Sabeans), those who believe in the One God and the day of judgement, and do good, shall be rewarded by their creator and shall not fear or be sad" (Al Baqarah 2:2–62).

Muslims are required to perform the five daily prayers and are encouraged to pray in a mosque. But on Fridays they must attend a mosque and listen to the Friday sermon before praying behind an Imam (prayer leader). The premise is that there is a direct relationship between a Muslim and his or her creator, and they can pray to their creator anywhere; but Muslims are encouraged to promote a spirit of community, hence the call for group prayer in a mosque to know and empathize with each other. They must wash their faces, arms, ears, and feet in a ritual of cleansing before any prayer and are encouraged to bathe before the Friday prayer and always after marital relations. Prayers do not take much time. In fact, if a person prays at home, it takes no more than five minutes, unless they are reciting long verses of the Quran. Each prayer reminds Muslims of their belief in the One God and their duties toward their creator, other human beings, and their environment.

Fasting the holy month of Ramadhan is a religious rite that is meant to have Muslims identify and empathize with the poor who have nothing to eat, and as a form of self-discipline. During Ramadhan, observant Muslims cease eating any food and drinking any fluids from before dawn until sunset. This can be hard, especially when Ramadhan falls during the summer, which is why Ramadhan nights are lively and people stay up late, sometimes until they have their last meal before dawn. Work hours are reduced to six in many Muslim countries, and the workday starts later than normal to allow people to sleep late, having stayed up late into the night. Ramadhan is a month of prayer, reflection, and charity.

6.

THE EID

"Wake up H'mad, it's Eid. We're no longer fasting as we bade farewell to Ramadhan last night," my mother was calling. "H'mad" was how Ahmad was pronounced in the local dialect. I heard the approaching sound of the Sultani Band playing and ran to the window to see the band marching up the street below, dressed in their finest uniform of khaki shorts and black velvet jackets, decorated with brass buttons and golden ropes. They wore beautifully starched Rajasthani-style turbans with pleated fans jutting from the top of each turban. I recognized Abdulkhaliq, one of my mother's cousins, playing the trumpet. Many children of the area ran after the band. I stayed at the window watching until they rounded the corner of the street.

I looked up to see the open grounds of the town hospital, much more peaceful than they had been two years earlier. I wondered about the children of the people who died that day and what became of the injured men. I also wondered at Father's decision to place me in the window to watch the gruesome sight—had he felt I was old enough to learn about these realities? I was seven years old on this Eid and old enough to start contemplating what had happened, what it could mean, and how it would shape my future understanding of conflict.

My thoughts were interrupted by the aroma of the Eid breakfast dishes that Mother was preparing. Lamb liver and kidneys frying in sesame oil with black pepper mixed with the smell of *shorkhorma*, a dish of fine vermicelli with cinnamon, almonds, and cardamom in milk. This was an Indian dish from Hyderabad that Grandmother had taught her daughters. The family gathered around a carpet of woven date-palm leaves laden with various delicious dishes prepared by Mother. Once Father returned from the Eid prayer at sunrise in the main town mosque, we sat and ate.

This was the morning feast of Eid Al Fitr on the first day of the month of Shawwal, after the end of the fasting month of Ramadhan. Children below the age of ten were not expected to fast, but did fast for a few hours; in other words, they were encouraged to fast but allowed to cheat. At puberty they were expected to fast from dawn to sunset, like any adult, for the full lunar month. As I was only seven years old, Mother suggested that I fast the last three hours before sunset when the fast was broken. The Eid was therefore a great celebration of old and young breaking the fast after having gone hungry and thirsty for 29 or 30 days, albeit during daytime hours only.

The new lunar month starts with a new moon. Therefore, on the evening of the 29th day of Ramadhan, many people keenly watch the sun setting and look for the faint crescent of the new moon. If this is witnessed by a sane adult male, the Chief Judge is alerted. He would then interview the witness and confirm his sighting based on the shape he described. If satisfied, the Chief Judge would declare the start of Eid Al Fitr and the end of the fasting month. If the crescent is not seen, the Chief Judge declares a full fasting month of 30 days and everyone would fast a final day.

By four in the afternoon, I was dressed in my Eid clothes along with my younger brother, Abdulkader (nicknamed Kadri) and sister, Khadijah. Salem was the fourth sibling, but he was only two years old and too young for the outing. I wore a nice red shirt, a beautifully decorated sarong, and put on my new rubber shoes for the occasion. (We usually went around town with no shoes, but my father decided to buy us shoes for the Eid. I remember him taking me and Kadri to Subait's shop to fit us with our first pairs of shoes; they smelled strongly of rubber.)

A truck from my father's transport fleet was parked outside the house waiting for us and our nanny, Sehala. Some neighborhood boys and girls were crowding around the truck when Sehala marched down from the house with the three of us in tow and climbed into the back of the truck to sit on the carpeted flat bed, like an African queen taking her throne; all this amid shouts of the neighborhood children asking to join the outing. Sehala selected ten or so children to join us, and the truck started down the street toward the sea, then turned right on the main road toward the town gate.

On our left was Almishraf, adjoining the Sultan's palace. Almishraf was a walled beach area where women went to bathe and wash their clothes in sea water. The Sultan's palace extended from Almishraf to the town gate, and on the right was the entrance to the hospital, which adjoined the offices and residence of the British Resident Advisor. Then came the Bagh, which was the Sultan's Garden. The truck finally drove through the town gate, a stone structure that was closed at night. As you came out of the gate you looked upon a dry wadi (valley), which people called Alaigah, leading to the sea on the left and heading inland on the right to join the maze of wadis that dominate the geography of Hadhramaut. I've since come to learn that the word "wadi" had found its way over the years into Spanish to become part of the of names of locations like Guadalajara (modification of Wadi Al Hijara, or "Wadi of Stones") and Guadalcanal (Canal Wadi). Alaigah often flooded after a good rain and carried flash-flood water from the many wadis north of Al Mukalla to the sea.

On the other side of Alaigah was a poor suburb called Al Sharj, which consisted of mostly hovels housing dark-skinned people that the townspeople called Al Sobyan. Most men of this area wore nothing but a loin cloth; they lived outside the social mainstream and occupied a low social status. My father told me that many historians believe they are descendants of Ethiopians from across the Red Sea who invaded Yemen in the fourth century and established themselves along the coastal plains of Yemen. They gained power and ruled Yemen as the Kingdom of Axom for around 200 years while spreading Christianity among Arab tribes of the area. Their rule did not last, but Christianity survived among some tribes.

Judaism had arrived in Yemen even earlier, in the year 70 A.D., as some Jews fled the rule of the Roman Emperor

Titus and sought refuge in Yemen. After the demise of Ethiopian rule, one ruler of Yemen adopted Judaism at the end of the fourth century, and Christianity and Judaism co-existed among Arab tribes. However, a later ruler called Yousuf Thu Nawas also adopted Judaism in the early sixth century and declared it the official religion of the land. He persecuted Christians who refused to convert and burned some of them alive in Najran (now a border city in Saudi Arabia). This instigated another invasion by Ethiopians in 525 A.D., to avenge the burning of Christians. They conquered Thu Nawas and established a kingdom that lasted until the end of the sixth century. The story of burning Christians is mentioned in the Quran. It promises hell for those who persecuted the believers for their belief. The Ethiopians were once again driven out by a Persian army that was sent by the King of Persia in response to a call for help from a local king named Saif bin Thi Yazan, who ruled the area under the protection of the Persians until his death.

The mainstay of Sharj was the production of sesame oil in primitive factories. Oxen or camels were used to turn a mill consisting of a round-stone to crush sesame seeds on top of a similar stone to produce the oil. Grooves in the bottom round stone directed the oil to a metal container placed just below the center of the stone.

Another specialty of Al Sharj was cooking *krash*. Al Mukalla was not only the capital of Al Qu'aiti State but also a major fishing center with a sizeable market where Indian Ocean fish of all kinds and sizes were sold. Al Sharj residents would pick up the entrails of large fish, cook them with spices, onions, and tomatoes, and sell them on the streets of Al Mukalla. I fell in love with the taste of *krash* and would seek out the dark-skinned man wearing nothing but a loin cloth sitting by the roadside with a black pot, knife, and cutting board in front of him, selling portions of *krash* wrapped in old newspapers. I would buy the *krash* and head to the nearby cemetery to eat it, because Mother did not approve of my taste for it. One day, however, she found out about my practice and decided to cook *krash* herself. She sent Sehala to buy the internal organs of large fish, picked only the liver and heart, and proceeded to give them a good cleaning. Sehala stood watching and shaking her head then finally said, "You can't do this. All this cleaning will not make it taste like the real thing." Mother's enthusiasm suddenly deflated, and she threw her hands up in defeat. But she never expressed approval of buying *krash* on the street.

The truck drove around Al Sharj for a few kilometers and stopped at an area called Ba'abood, named after the tomb of a religious man and built among beautiful sand dunes with clean white sand and steep sides. The screaming children jumped out and we spent two hours running up and down the slopes of the dunes, taking the sweets and drinks from the men selling in the area. At sunset, the truck was loaded and started back to town.

We drove past the British Commissioner's residence. As we were passing it, I saw a man with a pink face and short blond hair driving out in an open convertible. A very white woman wearing a hat sat in the passenger seat. I had never seen someone with such skin color; knowing the names of white people didn't mean we understood what they looked like in real life. My mother was considered white by her family and friends, but she had jet black hair and did not have the pinkish tint to her skin nor the blond hair of both the man and woman. I recognized that they were foreigners and wondered about the place they came from.

My brother, sister, and I were worn out by our day of running up and down sand dunes and fell asleep in no time. As I was drifting off, I heard my mother asking about my missing shoes. Who knew? Perhaps they may still be buried in the sand dune.

I dreamt that night of being with the two foreigners in their own country. There were green grass, beautiful trees, and running rivers, images I saw in books and magazines that Father brought home every week.

———

Our family was always invited to an early afternoon feast at our maternal grandfather's home on the second day of the Eid. On this day, my mother dressed us in our best clothes, then took her time dressing. She finally donned her *shugga*, which was the outer full covering consisting of a long black skirt and a short black cloak to cover the upper part of her body. She then covered her face with a black sheer cloth with red and white circular patterns tied behind her head before putting on a black head cover to conceal all her hair and neck.

In later years I saw this same cloth used in India in Muslim areas, covering the faces of some women. This way of dressing outside a woman's home was based on the conservative belief that no part of a woman's body, including her face, should be seen by strange men. Some groups of society like farmers, artisans, or fishermen did not insist on covering the faces of women but expected them to carefully cover the rest of their bodies. Bedouin women wore burqas on their faces that showed their eyes clearly but hid the rest of their faces. In some Bedouin tribes in Saudi Arabia, women never showed their faces except their eyes, even to their husbands. Some Bedouin men may never see the full face of their wives. Each group of society had its customs that it adhered to strictly; but it's hard to know how these customs started and persisted.

The whole family, including Sehala, walked the few blocks to Dada's home, where Grandpa lived with Grandma, two sons, three daughters, and three granddaughters. All attended the feast that was prepared by Grandma with the assistance of Ummi Boruka, the maid. The men sat on the second level of the house and ate there, while the women gathered and ate on the third level. Boys and girls are automatically men and women when they reach puberty. Men can only see and mix with the females of their immediate family—mother, sister, aunt, niece, grandmother, granddaughter, and grandniece; while women can only mix with father, brother, uncle, nephew, grandfather, grandson and grandnephew. In other words, both can mix with members of the other sex that they cannot marry.

The food was excellent Hyderabadi cuisine: Hyderabadi *biryani* (rice and meat with yogurt and spices), *bagara baingan* (spiced eggplant in sesame sauce), *dal* (lentils cooked with onions and spices), spinach with meat in tomato sauce, *kuchumber* (chopped fresh onions, tomatoes, and hot green pepper), and Hyderabadi *achar* (spiced lemon or mango pickle). Needless to say, I needed no encouragement to eat my fill.

After the great meal, the men chatted over some excellent tea for about an hour, then dispersed. My father left us to enjoy the rest of the day and evening with the family, and I went up to join the women and children. The children told stories and played hide and seek; but as the evening progressed, I found myself sitting alone with Grandpa. He must have been in his late 70s and in good health, except for a bad abdominal hernia. He had a special belt that compressed the hernia area in his lower abdomen and allowed him to move around.

This day was made particularly memorable. I was sitting by Grandfather when suddenly, he said something unintelligible to me. I looked at him confused until he repeated himself, but I still could not understand. Frustrated, he started to shout, and I ran out of the room to get my youngest aunt to see what Grandpa wanted. It turned out that he was asking me to hand him his set of teeth that were in a glass of water near me. That made sense—broken Arabic and missing teeth made understanding him hard. Though this was slightly frightening at the time, it gave us something to laugh about later.

I thought of him as a hot-tempered old man for a long time, one whom I feared. But when looking back I also remember him talking with my mother in an endearing way, often using the Urdu word "beta" which is an affectionate way of calling a son or daughter. Mother understood Urdu—an Indo-Aryan language related to Hindi but written in Persian script—as it was the medium of communication between her parents, but while her father did not speak Arabic, her mother spoke such perfect and beautiful Arabic that her father insisted on teaching her. She spoke only in Arabic to her children. Therefore, all of them spoke Arabic but only few of them spoke Urdu even though all of them understood it. This made Grandfather something of a revered stranger in his own home.

7.
DADA AND HABABA

Dada

We all called my maternal grandfather Dada, which was the Urdu term for "grandfather," but others called him Sayed Daud. We called my maternal grandmother Hababa, which was the local term for "grandmother."

Dada spoke broken Arabic, as he was born and raised in Hyderabad, India toward the end of the nineteenth century; one of his ancestors had moved from Hama, Syria to Iraq, then finally settled in Hyderabad. The ancestor was a religious scholar and preacher who traced his lineage to Prophet Mohammad through the Prophet's grandson Alhassan.

As a descendent of the Prophet, he and his male descendants carried the title Sayed, as tradition dictated. He came to India as preacher and Imam (prayer leader), and his descendants became Muslim Indians who were keenly aware of their heritage even as they lost their Arabic language competence. Dada attended Osmania University in Hyderabad and became an architect, just past the turn of the century. His second language after Urdu was Farsi, which afforded him a world of poetry and literature.

Soon after the end of World War I, he was contacted with an offer from Sultan Ghalib Al Qu'aiti, inviting him to Al Mukalla to build a large *masjid* (mosque) to mark the Sultan's reign. It was to be the *jamea* (main mosque) for Al Mukalla, where the Friday *Jumaa* (prayer) was to be conducted, starting with the Friday sermon. It was no problem for Dada to communicate with Sultan Ghalib then, as Sultan Ghalib himself was born in India and spoke Urdu fluently. Dada accepted the offer and sailed to Al Mukalla from Mumbai, where he was given (what they believed to be) a generous budget, and he began in earnest to build the mosque in the center of Al Mukalla.

However, when Sultan Ghalib suddenly died in 1921 and was succeeded by his brother, Sultan Omar, Dada's budget ran out. He had designed the mosque with two beautiful minarets but had only managed to build one, so he went to Sultan Omar asking for more money to complete the second minaret. Sultan Omar, who was known to be tight-fisted, considered the request then decided that one minaret was sufficient—and that was that. Today, you can still see the base of the unbuilt minaret, commemorating Sultan Omar's tight fist, and the mosque survives as Masjid Omar, which comfortably accommodates hundreds of worshippers every day.

————

Hyderabad was a state in the south of India ruled by a Muslim Nizam, the Muslim equivalent of Maharaja. He was apparently of Arab origin and his guards were mostly Arabs. Of these, a high percentage came from the Yafei tribe, who lived west of Hadhramaut. The Qu'aitis were a branch of Ya-fei who were prominent among the Nizam's army and at one point provided its chief commander. Such position afforded the Qu'aitis power and wealth, which they accumulated in the form of vast land holdings and thriving gold trade. They used their wealth to become rulers of Hadhramaut after de-feating the various ruling families along the coast.

There is a suburb of Hyderabad City called Barkas that was and still is mostly inhabited by Arabs who moved from the Arabian Peninsula. "Barkas" is the way the Nizam's guards pronounced the English word "barracks," where they lived.

One of Barkas's denizens was Abdulkhaliq, who came from Sanaa, Yemen. He dreamt of setting up a business in India and making a small fortune. His dream was fulfilled, and he settled in Barkas with a Hyderabadi wife who gave him three sons and one daughter. When his wife suddenly fell ill and died, Abdulkhaliq was in his 50s, and he decided to return to Sanaa, where he had a good inheritance of land and other assets to grow using his small fortune. He moved west to Mumbai with his four children and boarded a ship heading to Al Mukalla on the first leg of his journey back to Sanaa.

In Al Mukalla, he met and befriended a lonely 40-year-old Hyderabadi architect who had left a wife and a young son back in Hyderabad. In a matter of weeks, the architect asked to marry the 16-year-old daughter of Abdulkhaliq, who readily accepted, and the wedding soon took place. Having arranged the marriage of his daughter, Abdulkhaliq wanted to continue the journey home. But his young daughter implored him not to leave; and so, he stayed and died not long after, without completing the return journey to his birthplace.

———

Having completed the mosque, Dada went to Sultan Omar to bid him farewell. The Sultan did not want to lose Dada's talents and asked him to stay and, since Dada had a comfortable life and growing family in Al Mukalla, he agreed. In fact, deep down he did not want to go back to Hyderabad. Upon his graduation from Usmania University, his father had him marry the daughter of his best friend, a woman who had lost an eye and apparently had insufficient redeeming qualities for Grandfather to like her, so he thought this job was a blessing.

Sultan Omar eventually gave him a job and a house by the gate of Al Mukalla. Goods destined for the interior of the country were loaded on camel caravans at the port in the north-eastern part of the town and custom duties levied. The Bedouin leading each caravan received a *chetty* (tax receipt) for each camel load for which custom duties were paid; Dada's job was to check the chetties against the camel loads before allowing the caravan to leave the city. He lived with his family in a house built against the wall of the Sultan's palace and connected to the gate. It was in this house that my mother was born and raised as a child.

Dada managed his money well and retired comfortably. He moved from his government-provided house to a rented house in Al Mukalla while keeping a house in the Addees suburb, which he registered in his wife's name, for the family to enjoy in the summers. He also bought a small farm outside Ghail Bawazir that shared water from a nearby natural spring with other farms.

I remember going with Father one day on an outing to Dada's farm. It was a rough ride of just over 30 kilometers in a jeep over unpaved tracks, but I enjoyed the wide-open space of cultivated land growing different kinds of vegetables and local fruits, along with Dada's strains of tobacco. The weather was great for the gathering that Dada was hosting in the little house on the farm, but the most memorable part of that day was the painful ride back to Al Mukalla in the jeep. Motion sickness took hold of me and was exacerbated by the smell of castor seeds that Father decided to bring back from the farm.

Dada also designed and built himself and Hababa a tomb in Addees to inter their bodies after death, a structure that was completed when I was around six. To celebrate, Dada held a *Mawlid* in that area on the anniversary of the birth of Prophet Mohammad and served dinner to the gathering afterwards. Mawlid was a celebration of the birth and life of the Prophet, who was born circa 570 A.D., with participants taking turns reading his history and lauding his attributes. The reading was interspersed with chants praising the prophet accompanied with beating of round drums called *tars*. At a certain point in one chant, everyone stood up in respect for the Prophet while singing, believing that his spirit and those of his companions joined the gathering. Mawlid is standard practice in Muslim territories with Sufi influence. Sufism is a way to heighten one's love of Allah and Prophet Mohammad, the Perfect Human. It also searches for deeper meaning of the Quran beyond the visible text and is not limited to any one Muslim sect.

———

Hababa

Hababa is the colloquial term for "grandmother." For some reason, my mother and her siblings did not use the Urdu terms "Dadi" or "Nani," but rather the local term.

She was in her early 50s in my memories of her in Al Mukalla, and was always calm and serene. She spoke beautiful Arabic, having been taught by her father, and spoke it in a clear accent.

As the British were leaving India in 1947, war erupted between Muslims calling for the formation of the state of Pakistan and Hindu zealots refusing the idea. It was a terrible time full of conflict and massacres; many Hadhrami-Indians were caught between the two warring sides and could see no escape except to the old country. They boarded available ships to Al Mukalla and brought all aspects of Indian life with them. I grew up eating Indian dishes, listening to Indian music, and occasionally watching an Indian movie because of it.

Hababa was a young bride when she married Dada and needed female support. This she received from several older Indian-Arab ladies, who essentially adopted her. They taught her everything about cooking great Hyderabadi dishes, keeping house, and raising children. They were there to help deliver her babies and keep her company when needed. They also kept her Urdu skills intact. Whenever we visited there was always one or two of them staying with Hababa, keeping her company.

I remember one of the ladies opening a little can occasionally and taking out a tiny pill to place in her mouth. I learned later that it was opium, dried and rolled into tiny balls, to which she was addicted. Opium was freely available at that time and sometimes used as medicine. Poppy seeds were used as spice and sometimes boiled with milk, which was then given to young children to help them sleep.

Hababa had borne eight children for Dada, some of whom she had difficulty with; one of her sons died when he was a toddler, and her fourth daughter, Aamena (nicknamed Ammoon), was mentally disabled and suffered from what could have been a severe form of palsy (diagnosing was sparse back then). As she grew up, she lost her ability to walk and connect with other people. She spent all day listening to Indian songs played on a vinyl record player, one with a handle that needed turning to play the next record. As children we were always curious about the player and would come too close to Aunt Ammoon, only to suffer a sudden slap on the head, always forgetting until the next time.

After Dada's death later in Saudi Arabia, Hababa seemed to live solely for the care of Aunt Ammoon, which became harder as they both grew older. She doted on her daughter and treated her like a baby, refusing to let anyone else do anything for Ammoon until she quietly passed away in Jeddah. My mother, who was then a 60-year-old widow, insisted on taking over the care of Ammoon in the same way Hababa did and dedicated her days and nights to her care until Ammoon died.

Whenever I visited Mother, Ammoon was still listening to her records. I was married by then and had a son. When he was around a year and a half old, he loved to sit with Ammoon and share her mints, but one day he came too close, or perhaps he grabbed too many mints, and got slapped on the head. I turned at the sound and still remember the expression on my son's face. He did not cry, and as the shock of the slap wore off, he had an expression of wonder, as if he were saying to himself, "I thought we were friends!"

Another influential fixture of Hababa's house was Ummi Brouka (Mother Brouka). She was the maid and the nanny who had lived with Hababa for nearly 20 years, a teacher and confidante to my mother and her sisters before they married, and she routinely imparted wisdom and advice. She was an encyclopaedia of Arab proverbs, most of which were universal, like, "Save your white penny for your black day," and she always insisted that she descended from the proud nobles of a Nubian tribe. Mother quoted Ummi Brouka's proverbs until Mother died.

I remember Ummi Brouka in her old age when she had lost her sense of taste. She ate from a pottery bowl and used it to mix portions from every dish served, along with coffee. When she was asked why, she said "It's all going to the same place." She was incredibly influential for our entire household, but especially for Hababa.

Not only did Hababa raise her own children but two granddaughters as well. Her eldest son lost his first wife soon after delivering her first child, a daughter who was raised by Hababa. Another was a daughter of my second uncle who divorced his wife and ended up with a toddler three years younger than her other cousin. Through it all, she was always the same calm and serene person. Hababa was a pillar of our family.

8.

HADHRAMAUT

The British colonized Aden (and dominated the rest of South Arabia for 132 years) because of its strategic location near the Bab Al Mandab Strait and its naturally protected port. The rest of South Arabia, along with neighboring Oman and the East Coast of the Arabian Peninsula all the way to Iraq, gained strategic importance to the British Crown as valuable territories leading to its prize holding, India. Aden was classified as a colony of the British Crown and its residents were British subjects, while the rest of South Arabia was a collection of protectorate states. As colonial masters, the British kept the peace among warring tribes and introduced a civil service system and disciplined municipal government. All this survived the socialist governments that followed the departure of the British in 1967 until unification with North Yemen in 1990.

Hadhramaut became part of the Yemen Arab Republic then, but until 1967 it was part of an area known as South

Arabia. In addition to Aden, South Arabia had 17 different states, including four within the Hadhramaut area, and all states had protection treaties with the British Crown; the Sultans of these states were tribal leaders who evolved into heads of state. Hadhramaut stretched from the border of Oman to the northeast, along the Arabian Sea for nearly 800 kilometers, and ended around 200 kilometers east of Aden. It was bordered on the northwest by the Empty Quarter in Saudi Arabia.

Despite being close in area, Hadhramaut's four states were diverse culturally, geographically, and politically. Adjoining the Oman border was a small state called Al Mahra, which was inhabited by people who spoke a Semitic language older than Arabic called Mahri. If you listened from a distance it sounded like Arabic, but at close range it was incomprehensible to Arabic speakers. Most Mahris also spoke Arabic by necessity.

The Qu'aiti Sultanate occupied the bulk of Hadhramaut's area and stretched from Al Mahra' Sultanate to Al Wahidi Sultanate, another state to the west. Interestingly, the Qu'aitis came from a tribe called Yafei, which was not part of Hadhramaut; they were a tribe of ferocious fighters who conquered most of Hadhramaut, which allowed several well-armed Yafei families, including the Al Kasadi and Al Nageeb families and, of course, the Al Qu'aitis, to rule the coast and the bulk of the interior. This was helped by the pacifist nature of the people of Hadhramaut.

Some Yafei fighters went to India and offered their services as mercenaries to Maharajahs who hired them as palace guards and army units. (There is a story of one Maharajah who did not pay his Yafei guards, so they laid siege to his palace until he paid.) Some of them, like the Qu'aitis, commanded armies like that of the Nizam of Hyderabad and acquired properties to become feudal lords in India, with extensive farm holdings and thriving gold trade. Some became money lenders. All this provided them with the means to return and unify the coast of Hadhramaut under their rule. The Qu'aiti Sultan (Sultan Awadh), who unified most of the Hadhramaut coast under his rule, was both the Sultan and the commander of the army of the Nizam of Hyderabad.

To the North was Al Kathiri State, ruled by the Al Kathir family of the Kathiri tribe. Before the Qu'aitis built their fortune in India, Al Kathir also served as soldiers there and ruled most of Hadhramaut and the western part of Oman (then called Dhofar). However, they lost Dhofar to the Sultan of Oman sometime in the sixteenth century, and the Qu'aitis ate into their Hadhramaut territory. Until the British arrived, they were under constant pressure from the Qu'aitis and had lost much territory. When the British orchestrated a peace treaty, everyone was coerced into respecting it, with the Qu'aitis recognized as sovereign.

The fourth state was Al Wahidi Sultanate, which occupied the southwestern part of Hadhramaut. It was shaped like a triangle, with its base on the coast of the Arabian Sea and the tip located to the north near the border with Saudi Arabia. It was named after the Abdulwahid family, which ruled from the fifteenth century until 1967, when the British left and the Democratic Republic of South Yemen was created. It actually split into four separate states because of rivalry among different family wings then came together to form one entity near the end of British presence—but in the end the state was fully absorbed within the People's Republic of South Yemen.

The British didn't just decide to leave the area abruptly; their comfortable presence began to face true disruption in the early 1950s after Gamal Abdulnasser and his free officers overthrew King Farouq of Egypt. They adopted a socialist form of government and decided to lead a revival of the Arab Nation. Abdulnasser was a charismatic leader and a great orator who developed a significant following in all Arab countries when people yearned for another Salahuddin (sometimes called Saladin, a great Muslim leader of the twelfth century, A.D.). They had lived under the yoke of the Ottoman Empire for nearly 500 years, followed by years under ,British, French, and Italian colonizers. Hence the call for a unified Arab Nation resonated well with most Arabs. Abdulnasser called for the departure of all colonial occupiers and supported some fledgling movements that started an armed resistance to the British in the mid-fifties, in Aden.

More discomfort came from the United Nations, which called for decolonization around the globe. The decision to depart Aden and South Arabia was finally made by the conservative government of the United Kingdom to take place at the end of 1967, but early elections in the same year brought a leftist labor government, which decided to simply pick up and leave in July. For South Arabia, it caused a hasty and unorganized departure of British forces six months ahead of plan, leaving the country at the mercy of a socialist movement that swept all other movements out of the scene and declared the formation of the People's Republic of South Yemen in 1967, renamed the People's Democratic Republic of South Yemen in 1970. It aligned the new republic with the Socialist bloc, closed the country, and instituted socialist policies. The movement attracted some of the lower social strata in the north of Hadhramaut who felt a grudge against the higher strata, especially Alsada.

Terrible atrocities were committed against religious leaders—some of them were killed in terrible ways by being dragged behind speeding cars, and others were arrested only to never appear again; they were simply accused of being religious leaders who brainwashed the public in the same way that communists fought the church in Europe. These were not protests but rather an upheaval by the lowest social strata who saw blind loyalty to the new regime as the means to getting cushy jobs in the new socialist environment. Violence against the upper classes was a vengeful way to show this loyalty, since the leadership accused religious leaders of fooling the people. This lasted for around one year before the government became stable and violence was controlled.

Significant changes were implemented. All businesses were nationalized, including farms, and the land was distributed to the laborers who worked it, only to go barren in a year or two. The laborers had no experience managing farms, but the government also forced them to sell to government stores at unsustainable prices. No one was able to travel outside the country unless they were over the age of 50, and then only after providing a local guarantor of their return.

One was my older brother who managed to visit us in Riyadh. He had been working as court clerk in Tarim, and he related to us what life was like there. Soon after the new regime came into power, he and his colleagues had to undergo military training after work hours. He was also required to assume guard duty at government installations on some nights of the week. But on the lighter side, he also relayed strange stories. It was normal for him to go to the government store to buy basic food items like rice or flour, and once in a while, the store operator would add something abnormal—in one case, it was flashlight batteries. My brother would point out that he did not ask for them and the operator would say, "If you want the flour you have to take the batteries." They apparently had a stock to unload, and this is how they went about doing it. Such was the life in Hadhramaut during this time.

9.

HOME SWEET HOME

When I was born in 1947, electricity was available in Al Mukalla homes, but they did not yet have running water. My dad paid men and women to get water from the Jabia, a government-run water supply location. The men filled two large five-gallon cans and carried them balanced on a wooden rod on their shoulders while the women carried water in lamb skins on their backs, the limps of the skins tied with heavy ropes run over their heads to support the loads on their backs. The skin was filled with water through the neck opening, which was then tied with string.

These workers came upstairs to transfer the water to *zeers* (large pottery jars). A smaller *zeer* was set by the window overlooking the hospital, where the breeze kept the water cool for drinking, and a larger one was in the bathroom. They also filled a raised square metal water tank in the bathroom with a faucet for bathing. Water was piped from the tank to the adjacent kitchen. I saw health workers coming from time to time to test the water and ensure that it was free of worms or other parasites. As for toilet works, the building consisted of two parts, each containing two apartments on two floors. The parts were separated by a space of 1.5 meters that contained barrels placed under a toilet seat in each apartment bathroom. The bathrooms were positioned with the toilet seat (consisting of two cement slabs with a space of about 10 centimeters separating them, allowing waste to drop straight down to the corresponding barrel) sitting over the space. Washing water from the bath or kitchen was piped to a covered drainage system that ran in the middle of the street down to the sea. The space in the middle of the building was open to the sky and separated the two parts of the building but was secured with locked doors on both sides. The "People of the Night" came in trucks every few days and replaced the full barrels with cleaned ones. They were called "People of the Night" because they worked while the population slept and very few people knew who they were. I remembered a visiting lady gossiping to my mother that so and so's brother was one of the people of the night. It was not a good thing to be famous for, but still an honest, paying job. The apartment consisted of three rooms on one side of a narrow corridor with a kitchen, a bathroom, and stairs leading up to the upper level and down to the street on the opposite side. The kitchen was a small, dark space in the far end of the apartment. My mother used the nearest room as both kitchen and dining area instead, because she needed more space and the two windows offered excellent daylight. She cooked on round iron stoves where she lit charcoal and laid the pots over the embers. There was no refrigerator;

very few houses had them, and they were kerosene-powered. Like all Al Mukalla homes, the building was made of stones held together with *noora* (calcium hydroxide). Noora is a white powdery material that was produced by burning lime rocks in kilns east of the town. Ceilings were supported by imported wooden beams covered with palm branches and leaves, which were then covered and leveled with *noora*.

Our home was one of twin buildings with a large yard between them. The ground level of the two buildings contained warehouses that faced the yard, while the side facing the street had shops. The warehouses in the yard were mostly unused. This gave Father the idea of buying a cow and keeping it in the yard for a steady supply of milk. I must have been around four years then and do not remember the cow much, but my aunt, Khala Aishoon, would keep telling me a particular story years later. One day she was looking down from a window in Dada's home when she saw me completely naked, walking toward her, followed by my brother Kadri—and the cow trailing behind us. Apparently, Sehala had stripped me for a bath then got busy doing something else, after which I slipped down the stairs, followed by Kadri, to the street. I have no idea how the cow untied itself and followed us, but eventually we were all returned safely to the house by one of my uncles.

With the lower level occupied by shops and warehouses, the first habitable level was therefore three meters (about nine feet) higher than street level. Each side of the building had two stairways, one for each part. They were separated by the entrance to the space between the two building parts that housed the waste barrels. Each had a landing at the main door protected by a meter-high wall. When I was seven, I invented a game of jumping from the wall of one landing to the other, about a meter-and-a-half gap. One day, I missed and fell three meters between the two stairways—predictably badly spraining my ankle. As I sat there in shock for about ten minutes, my youngest maternal uncle luckily walked by and saw me. He carried me up the stairs to my mother with my rapidly swelling ankle. Khala Aishoon stepped in and brought a good amount of turmeric and sesame oil, applying both generously to the ankle and wrapping it in light cotton cloth. I only had to skip three days of school but suffered several lectures on what not to do by both my mother and aunt.

Sehala was a cuddly black woman of the same age as my mother. She was full of stories and laughter. She used to say that she descended from Sangoor, who split the sea in half. In the Quran, the story is told of Moses leading Bani Israel (The Jews) out of Egypt going east, when the Pharoah decided to pursue them with a large army. Moses and his people became trapped between the attacking army and the sea, so he struck the water with his cane and the sea parted, allowing him and his people a path to cross unharmed. When the Pharoah and his army pursued them along the path, the water closed and drowned them. In later years, I wondered if Sangoor was the African version of the Prophet Moses.

Black people in Hadhramaut came originally as slaves owned by the various rulers and other rich families; but with the arrival of the British and the signing of the friendship treaty in 1863, slavery was banned. Interestingly, the British were responsible for the transportation of millions of slaves to the Americas, including women and children, and did not officially ban slavery until 1833, when the British Parliament passed the Slavery Abolition Act.

Many of the slaves ended up staying on as servants while others went out and built their lives among the community, with some joining the army and rising in ranks to be army commanders. They rarely intermarried with other social groups because of the social customs ruling marriage. Sehala assisted with the housework and went out shopping for food stuff (a daily chore), but she was also the nanny, bathing the kids and putting us to sleep while telling us fantastic stories. Our home was full of laughter and much of it was because Sehala was naturally funny and did her best to make us laugh. She was a part of the family and left only when we departed Hadhramaut. She used to tell Mother that the family spoiled her for marriage, as she turned down many offers in favor of the comfortable and happy life she had with us.

There was a black couple, Mahfouth and Dokhne, living in a little room in the corner of the street level of Dada's house. They lived by making and selling *madghah*. This was dried tobacco mixed with charcoal ash, which some working-class Hadhramis placed inside their cheeks to satisfy tobacco cravings. Some years after Dokhne died, Mahfouth asked to marry Sehala, who accepted, as old Mahfouth's offer was the only one available.

Although she was my mother's age, we thought of Sehala as a big sister who cared for us, made us laugh, and told us bedtime stories. She loved us as her own children. Some summer nights we would go up to the roof and stay until it was bedtime; we children would feign sleep so that Sehala would carry us down to our beds. She would laugh and carry us one by one, tickling us once we were in bed.

As my father was a businessman who owned a fleet of trucks and sold rations and other items to the government, we were considered a wealthy family, even though we lived in a rented home. We never wanted for food or clothes and never felt that we needed more, but poverty was common all about us. I remember a distant relative of my mother visiting one day. I always knew her as cheerful and funny lady, but I remember her vividly telling my mother that she sometimes used a pot as a drum to sing and have her children dance so they would get tired and fall asleep hungry. Her husband simply did not earn enough to feed them. Still, except for famine during the Second World War, not one person in Al Mukalla seemed to die of hunger.

I tried once to contrast my family life when I was a young boy in Al Mukalla with the life of the family I built, having fathered five children who are all adults now. My current family is materially richer with more comfortable homes and has traveled all around the world. But I believe that I succeeded in maintaining the same values I shared with my siblings. Love and commitment to each other was a major value that was practiced but not necessarily preached, not only within our immediate family but also with members of our extended family. In fact, my parents rarely lectured us. We absorbed their values because they lived them, and I believe I succeeded in doing the same with my own family.

10.

THE NEIGHBORS

It is interesting how ethnic groups that were historic ene-
mies in their countries can co-exist peacefully under someone else's strong hand. Al Mukalla hosted people of various
ethnic backgrounds: Arabs, Indians, Somalis, and other Af-
ricans, all practicing various religions and joined to various
sects. There were Sunnis, Shiites, Ismailis, Bohra, Hindus,
Parsis… you name it. This was a feature of the British Empire that moved human talent from one part of the Empire
to another as needed. Still, the vast majority were local Arab
Sunni Muslims who accepted other minorities and gave
them space. There were mosques around the town but no
temples, churches, or even Shiat mosques.

The east side of our building had an identical apartment that housed a Hindu family for two years when I was
a toddler. The man was a government finance administrator
and a devout Hindu with a statue of his god that sat on

a shelf in the middle of the sitting room. He would start his prayers while bathing and continue praying loudly as he made his way to the main sitting room to complete his prayers in front of his god. This was all clearly heard in our apartment, as the wall separating the long corridor running along the two apartments did not go up to the ceiling. The Hindu family had two children who spoke fluent Arabic. The boy, Haresh, who was 12, and his sister, Sonita, who was 10, often visited with my mother. They simply went up to the roof of their apartment and crossed over a low wall to come down the stairs and show up to chat with Mother. She enjoyed chatting with them and learning about their life and rituals.

The town's jeweler was also a Hindu Indian called Kaku. He introduced the April Fools custom to Al Mukalla, and every year he would enjoy himself at the expense of the townspeople. One memory I have of Kaku's shenanigans was about a rumor that spread one year that a cow spoke to the butcher, who was about to slaughter it, and told him that she was in fact a woman who was turned into a cow by a witch who stole her husband. She asked that he help her achieve justice instead of slaughtering her. Sehala heard that the cow that was spared was on display outside the gate of the town and decided to go see for herself. She came back describing how the cow clearly had human attributes, like sad eyes that implored everyone to see that she was human. It took the townspeople a while to realize what Kaku was up to. But every year, there was another April Fool's story that got the gossip circles buzzing.

The neighbors in the adjoining part of the building were from one of the Sultanates to the west. They were memorable because of the father's name was Dinar (a currency name still used in Iraq and Tunisia); it was the main coin of the early Islamic empires, first issued in the seventh century by the Caliph Abd al-Malik ibn Marwan, but few Muslims know that the word derives from the silver "denarius" coin of ancient Rome. When Dinar was blessed with his first-born son, he called him Dirham (another currency name now used in the UAE and Morocco). The son's official name became Dirham bin Dinar (Dirham son of Dinar) which invariably drew smiles from people hearing it for the first time. The dirham was also minted by Umayyad Caliphs as a fraction of the dinar, which also derives from the ancient Greek currency, the drachma.

Living with such diversity has given me an appreciation for different cultures and customs, propelling me into a life of travel and adventure that I in turn passed down to my children. While deeply involved with our own history and culture, we are accepting and empathetic to other peoples and cultures. In contrast, I witnessed others who always try to prove their own cultural superiority, or those who rush to adopt other cultures, feeling their own is inferior. Living in the USA as a young student was a fantastic but difficult experience for me as I was constantly evaluating aspects of daily life against my own values, meaning that I had to make daily decisions to reject or accept new norms or values. This was hard. By contrast, I saw others who came with me making an early decision to simply accept new norms and values without question at the expense of their own, and others who rejected everything new while preaching the superiority of the values and norms they brought with them. In both cases, they each made an early decision and slept more soundly.

I started college in Saudi Arabia in 1965 at a newly launched technology college modeled on an American engineering college. The college made an early decision to transfer the first two classes after two years to US colleges for two reasons. The college needed time to build a robust bachelor program, but also wanted to benchmark the quality of its instruction in the first two years by monitoring the performance of its students later in US colleges. As it happened, all of us did well despite the culture shock. No more than two of us were allowed to attend the same US college, and I ended up at the University of Texas at Austin with Nassar, a longtime dear friend, in the summer of 1967. It was a turbulent time with the Vietnam war in full swing and US youth working hard in school to avoid being drafted into the army. The antiwar movement was very active and led by college campuses, and so was the peace movement and the hippie culture. It was also a time of presidential elections which were contested by Democrat Hubert Humphrey and Republican Richard Nixon.

The University had a host family program for foreign students with a local family volunteering to befriend a foreign student. It gave the foreign student the opportunity to interact with supportive Americans and get answers to any questions he might have (only male students were sent abroad as a rule at that time). I was fortunate to have a caring and gentle host family. The father was a faculty professor of American Studies who had a good career as a chemical engineer but decided to go back to college and earn a PhD in American Studies. The mother was an editor of children's books. They had three teenage children, Justin, Sharon, and James. Justin and Sharon graduated high school in the same year and Justin decided to attend a local college. Sharon, however, was attending the University of Michigan. I asked if Sharon was going to live in the dormitory and her mother simply said, "No, Sharon is sharing an apartment with her friend, Charles." I was stunned but said nothing.

This was the first of many statements and cultural differences that I had to process through my own cultural lens and experiences. Sharon was a nice girl, and in my book nice girls did not live with a man unless he was a father, brother, or husband. Yet, it was her mother telling this and obviously approving of it. Would I have been as open-minded, although not necessarily accepting of others' ideas and customs, if I hadn't had the experience of living in the USA and talking to so many diverse groups of people from all walks of life?

Many years later when my two sons preferred to go to college in Saudi Arabia, I did not try to encourage them to go abroad. However, I did ask them to seek higher education in the USA or Europe. I felt that living abroad for a more mature 23-year-old person is easier than for an impressionable 18-year-old, and they would greatly appreciate the experience and the fresh perspectives offered by living among such different people. As it happened, my eldest son went to the USA and earned an MBA while my second daughter went to London and earned a master's degree in microbiology.

They are not afraid to explore the world and test their resolve and beliefs every day while honing their careers. I am proud to have passed on the legacy of seeking diversity and exploring the world onto them—both of which I learned growing up in Hadhramaut and Al Mukalla.

11. THE SEA

I was born less than one hundred meters from the sea and my school was across the main road from the beach. The roar of the ocean was a constant sound in my ears; it rose and ebbed, depending on the time and season. The boys of the neighborhood learned to swim in the sea, and some claimed they could swim all the way to the cargo ships waiting to unload their goods. But my siblings and I were forbidden to go into the sea; Mother worried about many dangers, including undercurrents, sting rays, sharp rocks, and the rare shark. I, therefore, never learned to swim until I went to college. Mother gave in one day and let me accompany a trusted lady cousin of hers to Almishraf. This was a walled area of the beach adjacent to the wall of the Sultan's palace and just down the road from our home, reserved for women to bathe and wash their clothes. Mother's cousin had a load to wash. She would take a sheet of linen, soak it in seawater, rub it with a bar of soap, then twist it and beat it against a rock. She then rinsed it in seawater. I was about seven years of age then but still wondered if the remaining salt did not irritate her, or if she soaked the sheet in fresh water when she got home.

There is a saying that Egypt is a gift of the Nile, and it could be said that Hadhramaut is the gift of the Indian Ocean. It provided sustenance and a door to the rest of the world. When the land could not sustain its people, the ocean carried them to Africa, India, and the Far East and brought them back time and time again with new ideas, foods, and technologies.

An interesting phenomenon of the Arabian Sea (the part of the Indian Ocean stretching from Somalia in the west to Pakistan in the East) is Al Baldah season, which is associated with the appearance of the star Al Baldah. It appears in the middle of July, when upwelling of deeper waters in the Indian ocean brings cooler waters and breezes to around 150 kilometers off the coast of the Arabian Sea, offering a respite from the hot and humid summer days. This period has been celebrated for hundreds of years and is associated with the planting season. The sea also becomes dangerously turbulent, shutting down all fishing activities and causing a forced vacation for fishermen. To combat their idleness, a festival was launched in Al Mukalla in 2004 and became an annual event, bringing visitors to Al Mukalla and offering job opportunities to idle fishermen. An old myth that associated medicinal benefits with early morning bathing in the sea was revived and helped boost the festival. Of course, it's still dangerous to be out in the sea; many years later I learned of the drowning of a distant relative who was carried out by a strong undertow. Mother seemed very justified in her fears when I heard this story.

Needless to say, fishing was a major occupation in Al Mukalla. The catches from the sea fed the people of Al Mukalla and those in the interior of Hadhramaut. Most of the year, fishermen went out to sea before dawn in two-oar, four-meter-long *sanbouks* (boats). Some went deep in the sea to catch large fish like king mackerel, tuna, or shark, using strong nylon lines. Others went out during the day and used nets to catch smaller fish, like sardines. Fishermen would stop at the beach to weigh down their boats with round stones before heading out to sea, and the stones were dumped overboard to make room for the fish as they were caught.

The fishermen were simple men with little or no education, but they lived by a code of honor among sailors and grew up with the values of Islam. I do not remember interacting with any of them in Al Mukalla, but in the first few months I spent at my uncle's home in Jeddah I met some of them. Uncle's home was a stop for many from Al Mukalla who came for the pilgrimage to Makkah. Some stayed as his guests while others stopped by to visit and sometimes stayed for meals.

Fishermen's lore abounded with adventure stories. We heard of fishermen hooking large sharks and being dragged out to deep sea for a desperate and losing fight. One morning in school, while we still lived in Al Mukalla, I heard that a fisherman hooked a large tiger shark but could not run away from it. The shark chased him to the beach, overturned the boat, and bit off one of his legs. Though injured, the man survived.

The stories were always fascinating, especially to a

young child. At my uncle's home in Jeddah, two fishermen told us of sailing into the deep sea before dawn and being blown west by a strong storm. They were lost and could not see land, so they kept rowing in all directions as the sun rose until they were tired and dehydrated. Night passed, only for the next day to be a repeat of the last. Their boat drifted aimlessly until they were spotted by a British warship and picked up. They were promptly rehydrated and nursed back to health. The one telling the story said they were given a drink that seemed to bring their strength back quickly, which he thought must have been wine—forbidden to Muslims—but he insisted it was the reason the Christians that saved him were healthy and rosy-cheeked.

Hadhramaut had a very specific palate when it came to creatures of the sea, and this was reflected in what fishermen caught and distributed around the region. For example, only sharks of less than one meter in length were fished. They were cut in half, salted, and dried in the sun; they were hardly eaten fresh. This was called *lakham* and was cooked with rice or vegetables to add some protein and flavor to the food. Other large fish like king mackerel were boiled in sea water and dried into foods called *haneed*. There was also *bughzeez*, which was salted meat of large fish that was fermented in salt water then transported to the interior. This offered soft pieces of fish meat for cooking. Al Mukalla people never came near it, as they had plenty of fresh fish to eat and could not imagine eating fermented fish.

Most, if not all, of the dried fish was sold in Hadhramaut's interior. In fact, the people of Al Mukalla did not preserve food in any form. They ate fresh fish, meat, rice, and vegetables. Cheese or sausages of any kind were not produced. The only cheese some people ate, usually with break-fast, was canned Kraft cheddar cheese that some shops sold. One of my favorite snacks was dried baby octopus tentacles, a popular children's snack often sold in shops. Al Mukalla was also famous for its high-quality tuna, which was pro-cessed and canned in a modest canning factory in Khalf, an area in the eastern part of Al Mukalla.

In contrast, people of the interior were skilled in pre-serving meat and dairy products. In Tarim, many sheep were slaughtered during Eid Al Adha, the Feast of Sacrifice, that corresponded with the Pilgrimage to Makkah. Meat was dis-tributed to relatives and the poor, but a good amount was kept to be made into sausages that were called *mohshi* and used year-round. Father used to receive gifts of *mohshi* from time to time and Mother was, of course, expected to cook it. She could not stand its smell, so she would cook some of it once or twice, then toss it. When Father remembered *mohshi* later, she would claim it was finished. Once Father caught on, he kept his gifts of *mohshi* in the guesthouse, where he had a cook from Tarim prepare it. He enjoyed eat-ing it with his guests.

The traditional diet in the middle of Hadhramaut (Wadi Doan) consisted of dates, yogurt, and wheat bread baked in clay ovens. They occasionally ate rice with meat or *lakham*, but in Tarim you eat as if you were in Jakarta or Singapore. Having captured the hearts of Tarim men in In-donesia, Indonesian-born spouses of returning Tarim men brought their dishes of *gado gado*, *sayor*, *satay*, *nasi goreng*, and different *sambals*, among others. While in Al Mukalla, returning Indian-born women captivated Al Mukalla pal-ates with their Indian dishes. But in all these cuisines were fish—a staple of Hadhramaut cuisine.

12.

THE LAND AND
THE PEOPLE

Images and writings in different scripts are etched in rocks
all around Hadhramaut, which was the home of different
civilizations and religions for thousands of years. Its name
itself is quite old and its origin a bit of a mystery; many have
tried to uncover where the Hadhramaut name originated.
One story says that Hadhramaut was the name of a prince
who ruled a thousand or two years earlier. Another says that
it comes from the blending of two Arabic words, "Hadara"
and "Mawt." Hadara means "attended," and Mawt means
"death," altogether meaning, "The land that witnessed
death." This origin fits with the Hadhramis' belief that it is
the land where Qawm Aad (People of Aad) lived and suffered the wrath of Allah, having rejected his messenger, the
Prophet Hud (Hu'd), a story mentioned in the Quran. But
Hadhramaut is also the name of a famous tribe that inhabited the area for thousands of years and co-existed with other
tribes including the famous Kinda, who spread across the

Arabian Peninsula all the way to Mesopotamia.

And yet another potential origin relates to the land it-self. The word Hadhramaut is also the proper name of a long valley in South Arabia that winds its way from the northeast to the southwest then turns southeast to the coast and divides into many valleys along the way. If you fly into the interior of Hadhramaut in a low-flying propeller airplane, you are perplexed by a flat plateau that someone seems to have taken a knife and cut many valleys into.

For a long time, Hadhramaut had a stratified society. At the top of the social hierarchy there were three classes, the Sayeds (Alsada), the Shaikhs (Almashayekh), and Warriors (Alaskar). Alsada claimed descendance from the Prophet Mohammad and were religious scholars, judges, and teachers who kept certified family trees proving their lineage. Almashayekh, who were also scholars, judges, and teachers, shared the same social status as Alsada. Some Almashayekh families also claimed descendance from disciples of the Prophet including his successors, the Caliphs Abu Bakr and Omar. The third group in the top social tier were Alaskar, members of significant tribes such as Yafei, Nahd, Tamim, Seyaar, Seiban, or Bani Kathir. These tribesmen became rulers (Sultans), or military leaders and warriors. The next level was Alhadhar, meaning town people. Alhadhar were the merchants, artisans, skilled workers, service providers, farmers, and fishermen, and this level also came with different distinctions.

Then came the Alabeed, a class made of those who were former slaves of mostly African origin. In fact, Alabeed considered themselves higher in status than some of the lower strata of Alhadhar. In earlier times, when tribes were constantly at war with each other, Alabeed were captured members of defeated tribes who were enslaved and lost track of their lineage over the years. At the bottom of the heap come Alsobyan, who lived apart from the rest.

Outside of the social classes altogether were the Badou (Bedouins). They belonged to one tribe or another but stayed on the periphery of the social strata of town people because of their nomadic life—small groups of Alsada choose to be nomads and live the life of the Badou. Many of the Badou were nomads, herding sheep and camels and following the rain and grass for their livestock. Before the arrival of trucks, some Badou operated caravans that transported goods from the coast to the interior of the country. In fact, the first car in Tarim was transported on camelback, having been disassembled in Al Mukalla then reassembled in Tarim.

Badou men wore sheets of cheap but strong cloth dyed a deep blue. They used kohl as mascara and mixed the blue dye with oil to coat their skins for protection from the elements. The result was that they truly looked blue in all aspects.

While many of the Badou made their living transporting goods and herding sheep and camels, the bulk of the Badou lived in settlements outside towns and villages and lived on raising sheep without venturing far from their settlements. Their women dressed much like farming women but were distinguished by green tattoos decorating their chins and by their unique *usaba* (head bands). They also wore sombrero-like hats as they herded their sheep, but wider and higher, and they freely decorated their uncovered faces with mascara and colors, unlike town women.

This social order established who could marry whom.

Alsada could marry into any other group but would not give their daughters in marriage except to men of their group. Almashayekh and Alaskar held the same privilege but could not marry Alsada girls, and so on. The government did not enforce any of these norms, but everyone was informally bound by these social customs.

These class distinctions accompanied Hadhramis as they emigrated around the world. In places like Singapore or Indonesia that host sizeable Hadhrami communities, it is easy to see the subcommunities that exist within these communities. In Alsada subcommunities, men continued to use the title "Sayed" and women the title "Sharifa." Even today in communities of sixth- and seventh-generation immigrants you find a limited number of Alsada women married outside their community.

Such customs led to some significant friction within the Hadhrami in Indonesia in the early twentieth century when an orphan Sharifa girl was fostered and raised by a Chinese man. He agreed to have her married to a man of Hadhrami origin who was not a Sayed. This raised strong objections from some leaders of the Alsada subcommunity who argued that compatibility in Islam was a condition for marriage, and that compatibility of lineage was key. This was countered by other Hadhrami leaders who referred to a known saying of the Prophet Mohammad: "If you are certain of a suitor's piety and good values, do not reject him." Given that Hadhramis in Indonesia formed vibrant cultural and religious societies that published newspapers and magazines in Arabic, the issue of this marriage became a subject of debate for some time among the whole of the Hadhrami community in Indonesia and back in Tarim.

There was a contrasting case in Tarim after the socialist takeover of government when a member of Alsada who supported socialist principles agreed to have his daughter married to a black member of Alabeed class. His clan simply ostracized him. Such customs are gradually weakening in the diaspora, especially as some girls became spinsters waiting for acceptable suitors of their own social class. Such practices were not limited to Hadhramaut; descendants of the Prophet in the Western part of Saudi Arabia also insisted on the same lineage for suitors to their daughters.

While this is eroding over time, some families continue to abide by it at the expense of their daughters never getting married. Social change is coming slow to Tarim. Once the heavy-handed policies of the socialist regime came to an end after the union with the North, people happily reverted to their customs and way of life before social rule, because people will not accept change if imposed by force.

13. TARIM

Tarim is a major urban center in Wadi Hadhramaut. It lies around 270 kilometers north of Al Mukalla and about the same distance to the edge of the Empty Quarter in the north. In contrast to Al Mukalla's subtropical climate, it has a dry desert climate with colder winters and hot dry summers, which allowed for building houses with clay mixed with hay. The town was fought over by several warring tribal chiefs for around 200 years. Finally, three Yafei families divided Tarim among themselves, making it difficult for its residents to move freely between the three areas until Al Kathir prevailed and made it part of their Kathiri Sultanate just before World War II.

Tarim had an agricultural economy with farms along the valley irrigated by underground water. The water table was sustained by flash floods resulting from monsoon rains. The word "monsoon" implies torrential rain, but Hadhramaut's share of monsoon clouds was quite modest. It was as if the Indian Ocean would occasionally remember Hadhramaut and send it some monsoon clouds as an afterthought. Some years the ocean forgot, but sometimes the rain it sent was devastating, with flash floods destroying houses, people, cattle, and plants in its path. Except for green parts of major valleys, the rest of the country was barren. Though the settlers of this area are resilient and resourceful, these conditions drove many people of Hadhramaut to set sail for East Africa, India, the distant Far East, and the western part of what has become Saudi Arabia, for hundreds of years. But many come back, as there is an umbilical cord that kept them emotionally and physically tied to the land.

Tarim's economy had another and even bigger source of income, which was the money sent by its sons in the diaspora—most notably from Singapore and Indonesia, and more recently Saudi Arabia and other gulf countries. A good number of Alsada families in the diaspora built fortunes and established trusts for their descendants that afforded them steady, healthy incomes. Some built palaces around Tarim with grand designs, made of clay then coated and decorated with noora, which lasted for decades.

Alsada constitute around 15 percent of Tarim's population. Most Alsada descended from Ahmad bin Isa, who was a descendant of and only eight ancestors away from the Prophet Mohammad. Ahmad bin Isa was also called Almohajer (the Migrant) because he traveled around the Levant and the Arabian Peninsula, escaping the Abbasid Empire's hunt for members of the House of Mohammad, to finally settle in Wadi Hadhramaut, circa 1,000 A.D., outside a village called Tarbeh. Tarbeh is around 15 kilometers west of Tarim and where Almohajer's tomb is located. It can be seen from the bottom of the valley with around 50 bleached white steps leading up to it.

One famous Alsada family was Alkaff whose patriarch, Shaikh Alkaff (Shaikh is a first name and not a title) was considered one of the founders of Singapore, and his statue is on display in the National Singapore Museum. Alkaff Mansion is now a national heritage site in Singapore. His children and grandchildren built palaces around Tarim and gave them names like Isha, Almansoura, and Tawahi. They minted their own coins and built roads and schools along Wadi Hadhramaut. The most famous of the family was Sayed Abubakr bin Shaikh Alkaff, who was knighted by Queen Elizabeth II in Aden during her visit in 1952 for his many contributions to social and infrastructure development. Of course, Sayed Abubakr was a British subject, since he was a citizen of Al Kathiri State, a protectorate of the British Crown. One issue to be resolved before the knighting ceremony was his refusal to kneel before the Queen, since he only knelt to Allah and never another human being. (A compromise was eventually reached, with him placing one knee on a chair while the Queen touched his shoulders with the ceremonial sword.) Incredibly, Queen Elizabeth may have actually had a blood relation to Shaikh Alkaff if we were to believe a 1986 study by Burke Peerage, one of the largest genealogical publishers of the world, which claimed that Queen Elizabeth is a descendant of the Prophet Mohammad through an Andalusian princess.

For a town that had less than fifteen thousand inhabitants in the mid twentieth century, Tarim had 360 mosques, exceeding the number of days in the Hijra year (the Muslim lunar year). In fact, Tarim was a seat of scholarly knowledge of Islam even before Alsada arrived. After Hadhramaut adopted Islam during the time of the Prophet, he sent some of his disciples to teach Islam to the people of Hadhramaut. Tarim still prides itself as the only town in Hadhramaut that did not revert to paganism after the death of the Prophet, which strengthened its position as the leading scholarly town after the restoration of the rest of Hadhramaut to Islam.

Social strata were much more pronounced in Tarim than Al Mukalla. Alsada and Almashayekh were the top tier who supported and held each other in high esteem. Alsada treated Almashayekh as equals in matters of scholarship; many Alsada scholars studied at the hands of Almashayekh older scholars, while Almashayekh deferred to Alsada as the descendants of the Prophet and were in the habit of kissing their hands when they met. Alsada scholars would return the gesture when greeting Almashayekh scholars. Alsada's money gave them an advantage, however, when it started to flow in from the East late in the nineteenth century.

Alaskar ruled fiefdoms here and there. At one point, Tarim was divided in three parts, each ruled by one Yafei family in the late nineteenth century. But Yafei's influence dwindled with the arrival of the British and their support of Al Kathir. Other social groups got on with their lives as farmers, builders, carpenters, and butchers, among other professions. They also served in houses of the richer Alsada and Almashayekh. They deferred to the two higher strata and gave up the front rows in mosques to them.

Some of the wealthy men would take second wives from farming families in secret, and farmers were only too happy to be in-laws of a pedigreed man who would normally be well-to-do. Children would be raised with false names by their mothers until they reached puberty, at which time the father would have no choice but to bring them and their mothers in from the cold.

Tradition ruled the lives of Tarim people, with many celebrations year-round, mostly religious. A major one was the visit to Hud, where there is a tomb thought to be the resting place of the Prophet Hud. Hud was the prophet Allah sent to the people of Ad, who built a great civilization somewhere in the northeast of Hadhramaut, or possibly across the border in Oman. The Quran tells the story of Ad, who rejected Allah's messenger, Hud, and invited the wrath of Allah, who obliterated them with hurricane-strength winds. In a 1992 book titled *The Road to Ubar: Finding the Atlantis of the Sands* by Nicholas Clapp, he described the use of satellite imagery to locate what he claimed to be the ruins of the Ad civilization at the edge of the Empty Quarter, northwest of Oman.

People from towns and settlements along Wadi Hadhramaut would descend on Hud on the eighth day of the eighth month (Shaaban) of the Hijra year, led by the scholars of Tarim, to spend three days there to pray, celebrate, and bathe in a stream that flowed all year. There were traditional processions from some locations to others led on different evenings, ending with mass gatherings to hear sermons and stories told by venerable scholars. Some Tarim families maintained houses in Hud, which they called *khiders*, to use during the event. This practice is not known to most Muslims and is mostly joined in by people of Wadi Hadhramaut in the north part of Hadhramaut.

Then there is Almawlid, which is the annual celebration of the birth of the Prophet Mohammad, when separate gatherings of men and women are held to narrate the story of the holy birth of the prophet. His life is retold through chant, with the playing of *tars* (round hand-held drums) accompanying the chanting. Most participants know Almawlid by heart and join in the last sentence of each paragraph. Almawlid is celebrated in many parts of the Muslim world.

There were countless other religious occasions around the year in different specific locations around the town that spiced daily life. They are part of what makes Tarim so unique and yearned after by the people and families who have left it behind.

14. FATHER

Father was born in Tarim. He and his older sister were orphaned at a young age, their father having died when Father was eight years old, and brought up by their strict, traditional uncle. He would, for example, encourage the girls of the family to learn to read the Quran, but forbade them to learn to write, lest they use it to communicate with strange men. Once they reached puberty, girls of our family were confined to their homes and not allowed to show their faces in public, and the only men they could see were close relatives. This did not apply to working-class families, where girls had to work in fields and homes or herd sheep and goats.

As customary, when Father reached the age of 18, his uncle found him a suitable young woman to marry, and they had their first child a year later. She unfortunately died during childbirth, but the baby boy survived. He was my older brother Abdullah, born in 1933. The uncle's wife was childless, so she took the baby as her own. And within three years, Father married another young woman and later fathered his first daughter, my older sister Zainab.

They all lived in a house that was built by my grandfather and his older brother. The house had three levels and was built of clay mixed with hay—the traditional way for the area, considering the low humidity and general desert climate. Clay was a great insulator, helping to keep homes cooler in the summer and warmer in the winter. In contrast, it was not possible to build with clay on the coast because of the high humidity, so homes were built of stone cemented with noora instead.

Walls were thick to provide structural support, and ceilings were made of thin tree trunks or imported wood used as beams covered with mats made of palm tree leaves, which were then covered with the same mixture as the walls. Some rooms had the ceiling supported with columns of imported wood; large reception rooms were said to be *um arbaa* (of four columns) or *um sit* (of six columns), indicating their sizes as related to the number of columns used. The floors and walls up to a height of one meter and a half were covered with noora. It has been made for centuries like this: the base material is beaten with wooden sticks until it becomes extremely fine powder. It is mixed with water and eggs, then applied to floors, stairs, and walls. When dry it is polished with special stones until it shines like porcelain—very slippery when wet, you learn from experience—and lasts for generations.

There was a fenced garden of around twenty palm trees behind the house that yielded a good crop of dates every season. There were also a few fig trees and space to grow vegetables. A well was dug in the garden that provided water both for the house and the garden.

At age five, Father was enrolled in Ulmat Baghareeb, a one-man home-run school that taught boys how to write, read the Quran, and memorize some verses. He graduated upon reading the whole Quran and joined the only elementary school in Tarim at that time, called Al Haq (Truth) School. This was a project of the Al Haq Society, which was supported by the wealthy Alkaff family. He had to be in the mosque for the Maghreb (sunset) prayer then stayed with other children to read and memorize verses of the Quran for about one hour until the Isha (dusk) prayer. After four years at Al Haq School and learning reading, writing, geography, history, astronomy, mathematics, science, and humanities, he joined Rabat Tarim, the school of scholarly knowledge, where he studied various subjects at the hands of his uncle and other teachers. These included Quran studies and the principles of Fikh, which involved rites of worship and laws that governed daily Muslim life. Rabat Tarim was founded by a group of diaspora Hadhramis from Singapore, including Father's Singaporean-born uncle.

Father soon became a member of a select circle of very bright and ambitious teenagers who were exceptionally curious and highly motivated. While conforming to social norms, customs, and religious practices, their minds were wide open to new ideas, and they felt driven to advance and develop their society. The group was keen to learn about the rest of the world and the more they learned, the more they saw their society falling behind — mired with ignorance, superstition, and resistance to change. They pledged to launch an organization for uplifting society and addressing social ills, even though they knew that they were treading on sensitive grounds and could fall afoul of their elders.

Nevertheless, Al Ukhowa Wa Al Moawanah Society was born in 1932, founded by these teenagers of exceptional vision, which translates into the "Brotherhood and Aid Society." At 19 years of age, Father was one of the founders and was elected Vice Chairman. They started by going out to the desert and trying to educate the Badou in social norms and proper worship. They published a monthly newsletter called *Alikhaa*, ("Brotherhood") in January 1939. They had no way to reproduce the newsletter, so they improvised by using agar, a gelatinous material that was brought from Indonesia to make a kind of dessert. In fact, it is the same material used today in medical research laboratories to grow bacteria. They would pen the pages of the newsletter in black ink on white sheets and once the Agar gelled, they gently pressed the sheets on it for the ink to be transferred to form a master sheet on the surface of the agar. They would then place several sheets on the agar to make a few copies of the page. The content of the newsletter was handwritten in beautiful Arabic with unusually brave articles dissecting social problems, criticizing customs, or criticizing lack of government action, as well as articles discussing science and technology.

Incredibly, one article predicted the arrival of "pocket" telephones. All this, by a group of young men in their late teens. They launched a school they called "Al Ukhowa Wa Al Moaawana School" that had formal education not only of religion but also languages, mathematics, and science. They then launched an institute to graduate teachers in 1941.

One of the best written articles in their newsletter was critical of the state of the courts and the need for reform, and they could not believe it when the Sultan asked them to propose reforms for the court system. But they took on the job and came up with good recommendations including the formation of a Supreme Judicial Council to oversee the judges of Tarim. The Sultan approved their recommendations, and promptly formed the Supreme Judicial Council to be chaired by a prominent scholar and the Chairman and Vice Chairman of Al Ukhowa Wa Al Moawanah Society as members.

World War II caused the suspension of remittances from the Far East. This, along with a bad harvest and the disruption of marine transport, caused a severe famine in central and north Hadhramaut, which prompted the Society to seek donations to a food bank and set up kitchens to feed the hungry.

The British Crown Resident Advisor to the Kathiri State was taking note of all this and became alarmed at the increasing influence of this group of young men. It was not clear if he took any action; but suddenly, the members of the Society of Brotherhood and Aid met in 1945 and declared cessation of their activities, referring only to unfavorable circumstances as the reason for their decision. Everything came to a halt except for the school, and almost all members left Tarim to settle in other towns or immigrate to East Africa and East Asia.

Father elected to follow in his grandfather's footsteps and travel to Singapore, once the war ended in 1945. He first moved to Al Mukalla during the reign of Sultan Saleh Al Qu'aiti, leaving his Tarim family behind in the care of his uncle. Women rarely traveled with their husbands, who often took second wives while supporting their old household from afar. Father's reputation as an enlightened scholar and reformer brought him close to the Sultan's court in Al Mukalla, where he came to know the British Crown Resident Advisor. This Englishman happened to be an orientalist who spoke and read Arabic fluently and was drawn to the eloquence and intellect of this young man from Tarim, so he worked to dissuade him from emigrating and enlightened him on the business opportunities available.

He told him that the government had a program to send food assistance to the interior of Hadhramaut but lacked sufficient means of transportation. The government had contracted to import trucks to sell to businessmen who would operate them and pay the government back from the generated income. Father jumped on the idea with youthful enthusiasm, and within a year his small fleet of trucks was moving goods from the port of Al Mukalla to the interior of the country through dangerous unpaved roads that traversed mountains and wadis. Father would travel back to Tarim for a whole month every year to be with his Tarim wife and children and to visit his uncle, sister, close relatives, and friends.

Because of the rough terrain and primitive roads, trucks traveled in caravans for safety—of the trade routes, equipment, and goods—and for good reason. News came one day that one truck of my father's fleet was hijacked and robbed by the Badou. The army was mobilized, and units were sent north to fight the aggressors. This continued for a few months, with more hijacked trucks and some casualties suffered on the sides of the Badou and the government. The Mogaddam (leader) of the Badou, Banhaim, became a folk hero with poems written and songs sung in his praise. The town people empathized with the Badou because they knew that they were simply hungry; they had lost their livelihood to the trucks that rendered their camel caravans obsolete. A peace treaty was finally signed between the government and the Badou and the war ended. But Banhaim was immortalized as a folk hero. Less than five people were killed and none of my father's trucks were lost or significantly damaged. The pay loads of some were looted, but the cost was not significant.

Father rented a house in the east part of Al Mukalla which he used as guest house to his visitors from Tarim and those returning from the diaspora on their way back to Tarim. He hired a man from Tarim called Ramadhan to cook Tarim dishes for his guests.

Occasionally, Father took me along to the guest house. One day when I was around six years old, I found a shaving kit in the bathroom. I had seen men shaving their faces, and, lacking any facial hair at the time, curiosity led me to shave my eyebrows and the sides of my head. Father was shocked when he saw the way I looked, then had a hard time suppressing a laugh. He had to cover his mouth when he brought me home later, while gesturing to Mother to keep cool. Of course, her shock was even greater, but eventually it turned to amusement and laughter. It was then her job to tell everyone else not to laugh, which was awfully hard. But a great thing about hair is that it grows back.

Father never raised his hand or voice to punish or reprimand us. We grew up in a family and community where a father is to be respected and obeyed, and Father never lectured us on this requirement. Love was not expressed in words. I never heard any of my parents or siblings say, "I love you," but rather they expressed it in gestures, facial expression, and sometimes with a physical embrace. Perhaps learning to express our emotions verbally is something that we should have been taught, as it was sometimes necessary later in life.

15.

MOTHER

My mother was born in 1926, the fourth child and second daughter. Her father made sure that she was taught to read and write at the hands by a respected teacher who came to Dada's home to teach the girls of the family.

She was only ten years old when her older sister got married then moved to Tarim. That brought her close to her mother and Ummi Brouka, and she learned a great deal from both about life, cuisine, and housekeeping—all this during the difficult years of World War II. Just as the war was coming to an end, she was married to a local young man who had the lineage requirement and moved to live with him and his mother. Her mother-in-law's idea of a daughter-in-law was more akin to a maid to do all the cooking and cleaning, and to wait on the mother-in-law night and day. No fault was tolerated, and insults were frequent. Within a year, Mother had had enough, ran back to her father's house, and refused to return. She became a divorcée at the age of nineteen.

By then, Father had become good friends with her older brother and was a frequent visitor to their house. Of course, he never saw her or any of the females of the house; but he knew she was there. She had the advantage of being able to spy on the men from the roof as they spent evenings on the patio. Within the year, he asked to marry the young divorcée, and the 33-year-old man married the 20-year-old woman. A year later, I was born.

When a man asks a woman's hand in marriage, Islam dictates that her consent is required. In the case of young unmarried women, silence is taken as a sign of agreement, because the girl could be too shy to reply verbally. In fact, this license was often stretched, and girls were mostly assumed to agree. But in the case of a divorcée, she must accept explicitly, and Mother did, knowing that her future husband already had a wife. But she liked this cultured young businessman, having spied on his visits with her brother. Being a second wife was normal at the time, and in this case, the other wife was simply a ghost in another town.

Mother was a beautiful woman with jet-black hair and a light, creamy complexion, a product of her Syrian, Yemeni, and Indian genes. She had hoped for a daughter as her first born but was blessed with a son. For a while, Mother fulfilled her fantasy by dressing me in girl dresses that she made herself. She loved her children deeply and cared for them equally; but I always felt I was special to her as the first born. I could never forget her gentle hands running warm water over my eyes when I woke up with conjunctivitis and could not open them, or her expression of pride when I did well in school. But she also dispensed love with discipline. My worst punishment was her pinching the insides of my thighs when I misbehaved. Whenever she allowed me to join her on a visit to family or friends, I was always aware of her eyes following me around the room. All she had to do was give me a stern stare and I would immediately desist from whatever mischief I undertook.

She had high expectations of her children, who imbibed her strong will. We all worked hard at school and were invariably high achievers. At the same time, she was in awe of Father and never called him by his first name. Whenever she spoke of him with others, she used his family name instead of his first name. Outside his home, a man of the higher social strata was called by his title followed by his first name. That could be Sayed Mohammad, for example, if he were one of Alsada, or Shaikh Mohammad if he were one of Almashayekh. Another custom was to call a man by the name of his first-born son. Father, for example, could be called Abu Abdullah, meaning father of Abdullah. Many wives would call their husbands in this manner when addressing him or speaking about him.

Mother fulfilled her role as mother and house maker while showing proper respect to Father. He reciprocated with respect and kind words. I never heard a harsh word exchanged between my parents. This reflected on our relationships with others including our spouses and children, and perhaps instilled in us an aversion to confrontation.

16.

FAMILY

Kadri was only a year and two months younger than me, but he suffered from asthma and was made worse by the humid air of Al Mukalla. Mother was therefore protective of him and did not allow him the degree of freedom I had. Kadri and I played at home and fought sometimes, but I was always careful not to escalate our fights to Mother as I knew she'd always side with him.

We sometimes played with other boys of the neighborhood. One time, the boys proposed a game of spreading out and stealing sweets from the neighborhood shops, then bringing them back to share. Kadri and I would never dare do such thing, but unlike the other boys, we had money in our pockets, and we wanted to belong. So, we bought the sweets and returned proudly to share the goodies while pretending that we stole them.

One day my father had a friend visiting from Tarim. It was a wonderful day and I tagged along as Father took his guest to the truck depot. There was a beautiful convertible painted with beige and blue colors in wave patterns. A driver took the car out of the garage, folded down the top, and we all got in for a drive. As father and his guest chatted, the guest asked if Father loved his children equally. I remember Father clearly replying, "Of course, but one can't help feeling a little more for the one who is ill." I interpreted that to mean that he loved Kadri more, and I felt bad for a few days.

Khadijah came two years later, followed by Salem two years after. Khadijah was named after our paternal grandmother and Salem was named after our paternal grandfather. In fact, Father wanted to call me Salem in memory of his father, as it was customary to name the first son after his paternal grandfather (but only if the grandfather had departed). I don't know why his first born, Abdullah, was not given the name Salem, unless it was the privilege of Father's uncle, the patriarch, to name him, in which case no one would have contradicted him. Mother, however, was not all that keen on the name Salem for her first born, so she told Father that Dada, her father, had a name in mind. She suggested a lottery that would give Dada the chance to offer a name, and Father agreed. Father, Mother, Dada, and two uncles suggested names, which were written on small, folded pieces of paper, and placed in a bowl for Mother to pick one. Sure enough, Dada's suggested name won, and I was named Ahmad. This process was repeated a year later, and Dada's suggested name was picked for Abdulkader, whom Mother nicknamed Kadri. By the time Khadijah came along, Dada declared it was time to name her after her paternal grandmother; and so, it was inevitable for Salem to get his paternal grandfather's name two years later.

The morning of Salem's birth was etched in my memory because Khala Aishoon asked Father to take Kadri and me out of the house while she and a midwife tended to Mother. I remember Father leading the two of us by the hand and heading to his truck depot, not too far away. It had started to rain lightly but when I looked up, the sun was shining through the passing rain cloud. At five years of age, I had associated rain with full cloud cover; this sight had just turned my thinking on its head. I had a similar experience six years later in Riyadh when I was eleven years old and I looked up in the middle of the day to see a full moon. It was an apocalyptic moment to me, as I thought the world was coming to an end. I remember shouting to a man who stood nearby, "Hey, the moon is up in the sky!" He nonchalantly said, "Yes, what of it?" This puzzled me. Until then I had always thought the sun came up during the day and the moon came up at night.

Two years after Salem's birth, Abdulrahman came along, and Father named him after the uncle who had left for Saudi Arabia. Mother nicknamed him Dohmi.

By the time I was seven, I could understand a good number of subjects that adults discussed. One recollection was of Mother still carrying Dohmi and telling a visiting lady that she wished there were a way she could stop having children. But as we were preparing to leave Al Mukalla two years later, she was already heavy with her sixth child, Hamza. He was born in Jeddah only four days after we arrived.

Mother's older sister was a frequent visitor to our home. Her name was Aisha, but she went by the nickname Aishoon. We called her Khala Aishoon, with *khala* meaning "mother's sister." A father's sister was called *amma*, but the only amma I had was in Tarim. Khala Aishoon was always there to deal with tough situations that Mother found hard to handle, like bathing a newborn or tending to a bad injury.

At age sixteen she was married off to a medical doctor who carried the same family name and claimed descendance from the Prophet. He also came from India, where he was recruited to work at Al Mukalla's hospital. Having settled at the hospital, he asked for the hand of Dada's 16-year-old-daughter. Dada, being a descendant of the Prophet through his grandson, Alhassan, insisted on proof of lineage, and the doctor wrote to India to get it. It arrived in a few weeks, and the wedding was held.

The doctor's contract ended not long after his marriage and he was recruited by the Alkaff family to be Tarim's town doctor. Khala Aishoon traveled to Tarim with her husband on camelback, the only mode of travel then. Given the hardship of the three-day trip and the remoteness of Tarim at that time, the family sent along her second brother, who was 12 at the time, to give her some comfort. After a year in Tarim, the doctor brought her back to Al Mukalla, pregnant with her first child. He left her with her family and simply vanished. Years later, she learned that he ended up in North Yemen as a doctor in the court of Imam Ahmad, then the monarch of Yemen. By then, the family did not wish to have anything to do with him. His son would have loved a father in his life, but his uncles filled the father-figure role to a large degree.

A few months after Khala Aishoon's return, Mohammad was born. She never remarried and focused all her love and energy on raising him, with her father and brothers offering male support and guidance to Mohammad. His eldest uncle made sure he received the best education and later sent him to Egypt and Germany to become a medical doctor. His second uncle brought him into the world of poetry and literature. The third uncle was not much older and acted more as older brother and protector. Cousin Mohammad was ten years older than me.

Mohammad was a bright student. After four years at the Western Elementary School, he joined the Middle School in Ghail Bawazir. That was the first time he left his mother, which was exceedingly difficult for her. After graduating in four years, he joined the finance department of the Al Qu'aiti government.

I always looked up to Cousin Mohammad and enjoyed being around him and his friends; they would meet once a week in one of their houses. One home had a single portrait hanging on the wall of the guest room. It was one of Hassan Al Banna, the founder of the Muslim Brotherhood in Egypt. The Muslim Brotherhood called for the restoration of the Caliphate, which was an Islamic state under the leadership of an Islamic steward with the title of Caliph, a person considered a politico-religious successor to Prophet Mohammad and a leader of the entire Ummah (Muslim community). A succession of caliphates followed the days of the Prophet. The first four caliphs were selected by consensus of the people and were called Al Rashidoon. However, they were followed by dynasties with monarchs that assumed the title of Caliph, which became an inherited title and position.

The Muslim Ummah witnessed many of its golden days under the rule of these dynasties starting with the Umayyads, Abbasids, Fatimids, Mamelukes, and finally the Ottomans. The quest of the Muslim Brotherhood that sprang in Egypt in the early twentieth century was therefore a romantic dream to restore the glory of the Muslim Caliphate, which appealed to Muslim youth, including Cousin Mohammad and his friends. This, however, undermined the concept of Arab Nation, to be superseded by the concept of Muslim Ummah and the installation of a Caliph holding all power. This resulted in a clash with the Brotherhood by many Arab states. The Brotherhood was also accused of resorting to assassinations and sabotage to achieve its goal, including a failed attempt to assassinate Gamal Abdulnasser in 1955, the President of the Republic of Egypt at the time who had deposed King Farouk in 1952. The leadership of the Brotherhood was rounded up, and Al Banna's successor, Sayed Qutub, was arrested, tried, and executed that year by Gamal Abdulnasser.

I remember walking with Mohammad in the main market one day when he suddenly announced that we needed to go to Masjid Omar to join a funeral prayer for Sayed Qutub. Funeral prayers are performed as a rite before burial, with the dead laid in front of the faithful. They are also held in remote places in honor of the death of significant persons. Hence, while Sayed Qutub was buried in Cairo, his supporters held funeral prayers for him in many other locations.

Cousin Mohammad and his friends were simply attracted to a renaissance of a Muslim nation but had no thoughts of political intrigue or connections with the Brotherhood in Egypt or elsewhere. They shared this dream but had no radical thoughts about achieving it.

17.

EDUCATION

The school system in Al Mukalla was designed by Sudanese educators whose own system was based on the British matriculation model. Elementary school had only four years of study, with all subjects taught in Arabic. After graduating elementary school, students would then choose between a local religious institute in Al Mukalla and the Middle School, which was in Ghail Bawazir, 25 kilometers inland. With the bad road and limited transportation between Al Mukalla and Ghail Bawazir, the Middle School was a boarding school by necessity. It also had four levels, but the curriculum was intensive and challenging. Graduates earned a good level of competence in Arabic, English, literature, and the sciences, and were ready to join the understaffed civil services.

There were only two elementary schools in our town: the East School, and the West School, with the latter situated on the corner of the hospital grounds facing our home. When I was five, Father announced that it was time for me and Kadri, who was only four, to go to school. He took us on the short walk to the principal's office, who welcomed us with some sweets. We were then assigned to separate classrooms. After a week of bewilderment in class among classmates who were older, we both refused to go back to school. Both our parents accepted that we were too young for school and left us alone. Meanwhile, two female cousins, who were about my age, were placed in the only girl's school in town. On a visit to my Dada's place one day, I discovered the books they were issued and was fascinated by the interesting pictures of animals and other illustrations. I suddenly got the urge to go back to school and have my own books.

I was welcomed back in school, and it did not take me too long to catch up. By the second year, I was already reading and writing. In my third year, I joined my classmates twice a week in cleaning our classroom and the corridor before school started. I would then return home to wash and dress for school. My uniform was a white short-sleeved shirt over a white sarong that had a red line near the bottom hem, and a soft white round cap on my head. No shoes were required. During the school's mid-day break we went out and crossed the main road to the beach to play.

One game was to catch a snail and bring it back to class. I would make a paper boat and set it on top of the snail. Once the snail felt safe enough it would move, and the paper boat would float across my desk. Later in the afternoon we played *karandas* or soccer.

Teachers were strict disciplinarians who were free to beat their students. I was a good and well-behaved student but still did not escape a beating by the math teacher, and that was because I forgot to bring my pencil. The feeling of injustice for this inequitable punishment never left me, and of all my teachers, I only remembered the name of the teacher who beat me savagely on my back side with a long ruler as I was made to stand with my hands on the desk. I am glad such punishments were largely banned when I had my own children.

Skipping school was not an option. If a student did not show up, the school janitor would be sent to bring him. Kadri once played sick and mother believed him, so she allowed him to skip school, but it wasn't long until the school janitor showed up at our door. By then, Mother had realized there was nothing wrong with Kadri and she showed the janitor to where he was hiding. He picked him up and carried him crying to school. Needless to say, education was taken very seriously in Al Mukalla—not that some of us appreciated it fully in the moment.

The curriculum involved some classes in religion. One was dedicated to reading and memorizing some verses of the Quran, and another class was on methods of prayer and Islamic teachings of behavior in public life. However, we never had to pray in school, as we started at 7:00 a.m., and quit just past noon, a period during which no prayer was mandated. The five daily Muslim prayers are:

- *Fajr* (dawn) to be prayed before daylight.
- *Dhuhr* (mid-day) to be prayed within three hours from the sun reaching its zenith.
- *Asr* (late afternoon) about three hours after Dhuhr.
- *Maghreb* (sunset) within a half hour from sunset.
- *Isha* (dusk) around one hour and a half after sunset with several hours available to perform the prayer.

The highlight of my fourth and last year in school took place before final exams. It was the celebration of our completion of our reading of the Quran, which meant that we had fully memorized the 30th and last chapter of the Quran. The Quran has 30 chapters that contain a total of 114 Suras. Suras vary in length and number of verses. The content of the Quran was of three categories: the concept of unity of God, narratives of the early prophets, and ethical and legal rules. The narratives obviously claim a significant portion of the text and you find them in longer suras such as Albaqara. The yard of the school was carpeted and the fathers of the students in the fourth year were invited to this official event. Each of us was dressed in his best clothes and had brought a dessert plate prepared by his mother. The principal gave a speech, then we all took turns reciting one of the suras of the 30th chapter.

No higher education institutions existed in the whole of South Arabia or Yemen at the time, except for a teachers' college in Aden. So, bright students were often sent for higher education to Iraq or the Sudan. One of them was the principal of my school, who earned a college degree in the Sudan and became an athlete, specializing in swimming and diving. He demonstrated his diving skills to the Sultan during one Eid celebration by building a diving platform and diving gracefully into the sea. He thus became an athletic legend around town with a reputation that took on some mythical proportions. When there was a fire in Father's truck depot one day and men rushed to help put it out, a fellow student swore to me later that he saw our principal rush out of the school and leap over two men who were in his way.

I did not see my principal from the time we left Al Mukalla in 1956 until 2011, when he visited his son in Riyadh, and I invited him to my second son's wedding celebrations. He was over 90 years old but in great health, partly thanks to his athletic past. It was a very emotional event for me to have my childhood school principal attending the wedding of my son. When we chatted about the old days in Al Mukalla he told me that my father had asked him once why he was not married. When he replied he didn't have enough money to do so, Father told him to find a girl and he would pay for the wedding. This was one of the many things I learned about my father long after his death. Even before learning much about my father's life and accomplishments, I sensed that he had a distinct place in the community, and I always wanted to gain his approval and have him be proud of me. He was always a presence in my life, even after he died.

The world was not as physically connected as it is today, with limited mobility and communication with the rest of the world, but we were not isolated. There was no TV or internet, but we had radio and printed media. We had more time to read and appreciate poetry and literature.

As part of Eid Al Fitr celebrations one year, the Middle School performed a play at the Sultan's palace in open air. A stage was built in the middle large yard of the palace with rows of chairs arranged in front of it. Students from the Acting Club of the Middle School performed Sophocles's *Oedipus* in Arabic. My father was invited to attend and took me and Kadri along to see it. I still remember the scene when Oedipus punctured his eyes in extreme remorse when he learned that he unintentionally married his own mother. We were certainly too young to understand such a production but were still fascinated by the whole evening, and we never shied away from education or learning.

18.

THE BICYCLE

I was eight years old when my maternal Uncle Abdulrahman, who had settled in Jeddah, Saudi Arabia, shipped a bicycle for me and two tricycles for Kadri's and Uncle Abdulrahman's own son. Pure joy! No other boy had a bicycle in the whole of Al Mukalla, although they constituted a major mode of transport around town for men. Because of our tremendous fortune, the boys of the area gathered around us to view the wonderful gifts.

My brother and cousin happily rode their tricycles in the street, but I just stood there next to my bicycle, having never learned to ride one. One of the boys told me to mount the bicycle and he would push me, so I got on the bicycle as two boys held it upright then pushed me. Well, I went forward about two meters before falling, just as my mother looked down from her window. She immediately called the teenage son of our neighbors and asked him to bring the bicycle up the stairs to the apartment level. That left me embarrassed and heartbroken. The next day I sneaked the bicycle down the stairs and tried again, only to run against the house wall and badly scrape my right arm. Once again, the bicycle was taken up the stairs. Mother felt my pain and asked Father to have someone teach me to ride. Sure enough, a trusted employee of my father showed up the next day after school and walked me and the bicycle to Alaigah.

Everyone called the man Baatwa, which was his family name. Baatwa was a simple and good-natured man with a dollar-size scar on his cheek from a past *Leishmania* parasitic infection transmitted through a sand fly bite. He told me to ride and pedal slowly while he held the bicycle by the seat. I started pedaling slowly but as I gained confidence I started to speed up and the poor man had to run behind me holding the bicycle upright until he ran out breath. His effort was not in vain, however; it did not take long for me to get the hang of riding the bicycle, to both Baatwa and Father's relief.

The bicycle opened the world to me. Until then, I circulated only within 200 meters from our home and only went beyond in the company of a family adult; but no longer. Soon after returning from school the family would gather for the main meal of the day, then I would take off on the bicycle to discover every part of town. As I rode northeast along the main road bordering the beach, I would pass the tomb of Waliah Alawia (Saint Alawia) on the left, then Al-rawdha mosque on the right, which was built on the shore with waves constantly lapping at its southern wall. "Wali" for man, and "waliah" for woman, were titles given posthumously to pious individuals who devoted their lives to the service of Allah and the people around them. There was no authority that granted the title; it was rather bestowed by consensus of the people who attributed some *karamat* (minor miracles) to the wali or waliah.

As I pedaled, the Markeet (the fish, vegetable, and meat market) would show up on my left. Markeet was, of course, an adoption of the English word "market." Many other English words became local terms, such as graish boy (garage boy), rubbish, moter (motor), and baib (pipe), among many others. Interestingly, the common word for shirt in Hadhramaut was "chemise," which was French. As I got better at riding, my mother would send me sometimes to buy vegetables in the Markeet, so I became very familiar with it.

A little farther along I would come upon Mohammad Abdulaziz's café, where men enjoyed their tea in the afternoon. The café was on the left side of the road facing the sea but had some tables and chairs on the right side of the road overlooking the beach with a lovely view, especially at sunset. There was a square on the left past the café where Masjid Omar was located (Al Mukalla's main mosque) This area of Al Mukalla was called Alhara. Continuing northeast along the main road, the sea went out of view as two-story buildings rose on the right side. This was now the main commercial area, with shops on both sides selling dry food stuff, spices, and clothes.

You could often see boys gathering outside one of the shops on the main street, where they sat listening to the owner read stories of the heroics of Antar bin Shaddad and Abu Zaid Al Hilali from the yellow pages of old books. The man read in a dramatic way, with his voice rising and falling to match the turn of events, with significant pauses at the right places. The boys sat open-mouthed and wide-eyed in front of him, enthralled and hardly paying attention to anything around them.

I would cycle past all types of shops until I came to a square and the road forked right, going past government offices until it reached the port, where customs offices were located. Except for relatively small sailing ships that could dock by the modest pier, all ships moored in deep water off the port. They unloaded their cargo either to *sanabeek* (launches) that brought them to the port, or to *zaymas*, which were larger wooden ships that could dock at the pier.

Farther northeast was an area of Al Mukalla called Al-bilad, which was a peninsula that jutted into the Arabian Sea and was mostly inhabited by fishermen, and to the right was Yaqoub, the main cemetery of Al Mukalla. Then came Khalf—literally meaning rear—outside the town where the area between the mountain and the sea narrowed and filled with boulders. There I would often watch men coated in white powder from burning lime rocks in furnaces to produce the noora used in every house's construction.

But my favorite times were going down from Assiddeh (the gate) to the west down to Alaigah where there would be very few people walking. I would ride as fast as I could, the wind caressing my face, before slowing down to take in the scenery. The valley would widen as I rode north, and I would feel as free as a bird. After a good rain, the valley would flood, but as the water receded there would be half-meter-wide dry tracks where pedestrians walked. I loved the challenge of riding along these tracks without falling and maneuvering the bicycle around the few pedestrians who would be in my path.

One day, a maneuver landed me on my side in the mud, dirtying myself very noticeably. I picked myself up and rode straight home. Fearing my mother's fury, I discovered with great relief that she was entertaining some women visitors, which allowed me to sneak into the boys' room and change clothes without notice. I saw my mother smiling and shaking her head as she was picking up my muddy clothes the following day, but she never said a word. I made tighter turns from there on out.

I was returning from my Alaigah excursion one day when I noticed a large number of sardines on the beach, much more than I had ever seen before, with a fisherman unloading even more from his boat. I also saw some women helping themselves to some of the sardines to take home—not that it made a dent in the number of sardines available. I asked Father that evening and learned that it was sardine season, and the fishermen were contracted to fish the sardines and leave them on the beach to dry (called "*wezeef*"). They were then taken to be used as fertilizer by tobacco growers, which I would come to realize was a very impactful industry along the coast of Hadhramaut and in my early years. The sardines were so plentiful in season that families were welcome to take what they needed at no charge.

Enjoying the freedom of roaming the town made me yearn for more and I started to dream of traveling the world to see how different it was and how other peoples lived.

Smells are etched in a person's memory forever. One of them is the smell of sardines grilled in *tinnar* (charcoal ovens) when I walked the narrow streets of Alhara. The *tinnar* was an oven consisting of a clay tube of half-meter diameter and about 70 centimeters high, surrounded by dried clay about 20 centimeters deep and covered by a metal disk. The sardines would be skewered, and the rods placed upright over charcoal embers.

Sometimes, they would be embers of dried camel dung. I noticed some women collecting camel dung in Alaigah and mentioned it to Mother later. She told me that the women were poor and could not afford the cost of good charcoal. However, camel dung offered a good substitute, except for the bad smell when it was first lit. The smell dissipated once the dung turned to embers.

Another smell I came to hate was the stench of raw eggs. Al Mukalla was a tight-knit town and Mother never worried about me, which is why she gradually let me venture out into the town as I grew older. On some mornings, she would give me some money to get eggs from the small shacks up the mountain side where ladies raised chickens. I would walk around the area shouting "Shee Baidh?" meaning "Any eggs?" Eventually, a lady would come out of her house and call me to get the eggs, which I would carry back in my head cap. One day I slipped going up the stairs of the house and all the eggs broke, making me sick with their raw egg smell. I still get a little nauseous when I smell raw eggs.

I was a happy child with a loving family in a safe town with much to do. Although society was stratified with marked social classes, the people of Al Mukalla mixed daily, with few social barriers. All children played in the street with no distinction of wealth or class.

One sport I enjoyed playing with the boys of our area was called *karandas*. Years later, when I went to study in the USA, I discovered that it was basically American baseball with one variation: there was no pitcher. The boy with the bat threw the ball in the air, then hit it hard as it came down. Otherwise, all the rules were the same. I read a great deal about baseball in *Almokhtar* magazine, the monthly translation of *Reader's Digest*, learning that it was the primary sport in American culture without understanding the rules of the game. Years later when I finally watched a game on TV after arriving in the USA, it was something of a shock to realize that it was the same game I played as a child. Of course, our ball was an old sock stuffed with rags, and the bat was a flat piece of wood that we fashioned from discarded wooden crates, but the spirit was there.

Though we were just young children, the games could still hurt if you weren't careful. I returned home late in the afternoon one day and was confronted with Mother's questions about hurting another boy. His mother had come to our house complaining to my mother that I hit her son in the face with a stick. Earlier, it had been my turn to hold the bat and I swung it as I threw the ball up in the air, hitting the boy's face who had foolishly stood to the right of me, unseen. He was shocked and apparently hurt—but not badly. My mother apologized and gave the boy's mother some money; the poor woman simply saw an opportunity to get something for it. Afterward, Mother just said to be sure not to hit anyone again.

There was a small square structure n with a dome and four open sides, near our playing grounds against the wall of the cemetery. A small pool of water inside the structure was replenished every day by water carriers for passersby to drink, using an aluminum mug. What etched this structure in my memory was the writing in charcoal on the dome. It read "Ana Booseti," which was colloquial Arabic that translated into "I am my bottom." Even at eight years of age, I wondered if it was a joke or a statement that carried a deeper philosophical meaning. The phrase lodged itself deep in my memory. But it would creep up during in gatherings or business meetings years later, when someone made an asinine statement.

19.

A WINDOW INTO
THE WORLD

Father would walk in from work every Thursday with a stack of magazines under his arm. The first child to see him would shout "Ana Awal," meaning "I am first," and would grab the magazines, which usually consisted of the Arabic version of *Mickey Mouse* magazine and *Sameer*, an Egyptian children's magazine. There would also be *Almusawwar*, an Egyptian magazine and *Rose Al Yousef*, an Egyptian sociopolitical weekly. Once a month, the stack would include *Al Hilal*, a monthly literary magazine and *Al Mokhtar*, the exact translation of the American *Reader's Digest*. Then we children would establish the reading sequence with shouts of "Baadak," meaning "after you." The first child would select the most popular magazine, the next would pick up another, and so on. I read everything, including the novels, which were not always meant for children.

Every *Reader's Digest* issue had a summary of a popular American novel at the time, offering me a peek into life in

America, with some aspects distorted by the quality of the translation. One memorable novel was about a boy and his father who owned a hot dog stand. The translation said the father owned a restaurant that served hot dogs, leaving me with the understanding that Americans ate actual dogs. I finally had this misconception corrected by my American teacher in my last year of high school English. With every morsel of knowledge that I ingested every week, my hunger for learning about the world and the universe steadily increased. At the same time, my mind began to fill with questions.

Quran studies at school inflamed my curiosity about the universe with verses like:

- "It is He who created for you everything on earth, then turned to the heaven, and made them seven heavens. And He is aware of all things" (Albaqara 2:2–29).
- "So, He completed them as seven universes in two days, and He assigned to each universe its laws. And We decorated the lower universe with lamps, and for protection. That is the design of the Almighty, the All-Knowing" (Fusilat 24:41–12).
- "God is He Who created seven heavens, and their like of earth. The command descends through them, so that you may know that God is Capable of everything, and that God encompasses everything in knowledge" (Altalaq 28:65–12).

I once stared at the mid-day sun, and suddenly it looked to me like a hole in the sky. This led me to believe that if

I stared long enough, I could see into the next sky, which could be another universe. I did this repeatedly and it was a miracle that I did not lose my eyesight then, although this might have led to my myopia later and glaucoma in my fifties.

Over the years, when life allowed time for reflection, I tried without success to relate these verses to scientific theories or discoveries. But occasionally I would read someone discovering a text of the Quran that converges with a scientific fact or theory. One is a verse in Surat Al Anbiya (17:21–30) that states that the heavens and the earth were one lump as if sewn together, then God broke them apart which seems to converge with the Big Bang theory. Another verse to contemplate is in Surat Alanbiya (17:21–104) which talks about the day when God folds the heavens like a manuscript and recreates the universe. This seems to converge with a theory that says the universe has been expanding since the Big Bang but will eventually halt and fold back on itself.

I enjoyed being with Father when he regularly tuned his radio to the BBC Arabic channel. I would occasionally listen intently to news of the world, but my mind always wandered, thinking about how sound traveled from the BBC studio in London to my father's radio. This is how I eventually learned about the goings-on in our own home, our own region of the world, and it inspired me to seek answers to the many questions that began swirling in my head.

I never learned to share my thoughts with anyone, including my father. I am not sure why. Perhaps I just felt that my thoughts were mine to keep to myself, or perhaps I was not keen on being told not to think this or that, even though my father was open-minded and would have probably welcomed any curiosity. I occasionally asked a question but mostly tried to search for answers on my own. This early seeking behavior led me through the rest of my life.

20.

THE ARAB WORLD

Almosawwar was a weekly current affairs magazine with color illustrations and photos that I read thoroughly. My reading ability was already good at age seven, and the magazine gave me my early education in Arab and world affairs.

This was 1954, and World War II had concluded only nine years earlier. There was hardly any mention of the war in the magazine, except for the occasional WWII mine blowing someone's leg off in the Egyptian Western Sahara. It seemed the world was looking forward with hope and trying to forget the pain and suffering of war. The Arab world was slowly waking up and moving from under the colonial weight of Britain and France, and the United Nations was taking shape as a respected world forum and strongly pushing for decolonization around the world. While young and impressionable, I learned a great deal about the political and societal intricacies of our slice of the Earth.

West of the Red Sea was Egypt and the Sudan. The

British granted Egypt independence in a 1922 treaty, albeit nominal, as their army continued to occupy it until 1936, when the British withdrew to the Suez Canal area. The larger territory of the Sudan was made to be a joint colony of both Egypt and Britain until it was granted independence in 1956.

Egypt was the star of the Arab world, leading with its thriving economy and its vibrant cultural scene. Um Kalthoom was the paramount Arab singer whose concerts were tuned in to by most Arabs from Morocco to Iraq, and Egyptian films graced the screens of cinemas across the Arab World. We read intellectual works by Taha Hussain, Abbas Mahmoud Al Akkad, and novels by Tawfiq Al Hakeem and Naguib Mahfouz (Nobel Laureate in later years). Youth aspired to study in Egyptian universities, and affluent newly married couples went to Egypt for their honeymoon.

Having signed a treaty with Britain in 1936 shedding British domination under a protection treaty, Egypt became a kingdom with a democratically elected government, a constitution, and an active parliament, albeit still aligned with Britain as per the terms of the 1936 friendship treaty. When the Zionist movement in Palestine declared the formation of the state of Israel in 1948 and the United Nations decided to partition Palestine between the Zionists and Palestinians, Egypt led the opposition to this decision and the war against the Zionist state. Arab armies lost the war and much of the territory that would have been part of the Palestinian entity, according to the UN partition decision, and they accepted cessation of hostilities along an armistice line in 1948.

Much was made later of a scandal in Egypt involving corruption in the importing of faulty arms from Europe, suggesting this was the cause of the defeat. It was used as justification for the overthrow of King Farouq, later in 1952. The bloodless coup that brought the Free Officers to rule Egypt was a significant event in the history of the area that rippled across the Arab World with tragic consequence.

Officers are generally trained to organize and promote discipline for the purpose of waging war, but not to lead and manage the affairs of state. Gamal Abdulnasser, who led the Free Officers movement and finally took over as sole leader of Egypt, was a gifted and charismatic orator who impassioned crowds. He pushed for building the Aswan Dam as a strategic national project to generate electricity and control flooding of the Nile basin, but the World Bank, which had considered financing the project, suddenly withdrew its support under pressure from the US government. This was unfortunate, as the Soviet Union stepped forth with an offer to build the dam and sucked Egypt into the arms of the Eastern Camp. This led to the adoption of a totalitarian, socialist system that stunted economic growth for years and reversed many gains in social and political development with much damage to civil liberties.

Though Egypt was under the spotlight most of this time and appeared in newspapers daily, it was not the only Arab nation rapidly developing and changing during such a transitive time in history. Just north of us was Saudi Arabia, whose founder, King Abdulaziz, had died the year before to be succeeded by his eldest surviving son, King Saud, who ruled a population of around 3.5 million people. Oil was being sold at around three US dollars a barrel, but it was already generating good income for development and many attractive investment and job opportunities.

Oman, to the East of Hadhramaut, was ruled by a despot called Taimur bin Said under a protection treaty with Britain. He was not in favor of social or economic development, even though oil was starting to generate good income, and kept the country in a backward and poor state. Many of the fishermen and street cleaners in Saudi Arabia were Omanis at that time.

On the other side, to the west, was Yemen. It had a bigger population than Saudi Arabia but was ruled by Iman Ahmad, another despot who cared more about collecting taxes than promoting education and health services. The eastern part of the Arabian Peninsula north of Oman was a collection of states governed by tribal leaders under protection treaties with the British Crown. These coagulated into a loose federation called the Trucial States, which evolved into the United Arab Emirates of today. Qatar, Bahrain, and Kuwait were also British protectorates bordering Saudi Arabia and stretching along the coast of the gulf.

North of Kuwait was the Kingdom of Iraq. Its monarch was King Faisal II, who became king of Iraq at the age of three after the sudden death of his father in a car accident. The country was ruled by his maternal uncle Abdulilah as regent until Faisal II acceded to the throne in 1953. He was the third and last in a line of kings of Iraq that started with his grandfather, Faisal the First. Similar was the case in Jordan, where the Hashemite Kingdom of Jordan was ruled by King Hussain, who was the third in a line of kings starting with his grandfather Abdullah. In a somewhat similar case, King Hussain acceded to the throne at a young age after a short rule by his father, Talal, who was removed due to mental illness.

King Abdullah the First of Jordan and King Faisal the First of Iraq were sons of Sharif Hussein bin Ali, the Sharif of Makkah, and later King of Hejaz. Sharif Hussein was appointed by the Ottoman Sultan as Sharif of Makkah until he led the Arab revolution against Ottoman rule with the support of the British on the promise of supporting his quest to be the King of all Arabs. With the defeat of the Ottoman empire in World War I, he declared himself King of Hejaz and his sons Abdullah and Faisal were made kings of Jordan and Iraq, all with the support of the British. But he was something of a tyrant and unpopular among the elite families of the Hejaz and was forced to abdicate to his oldest son, Ali, in 1924, who ruled for less than a year. He lost his kingdom to King Abdulaziz Al Saud in 1925, who swept from the east and took Hejaz to eventually form the Kingdom of Saudi Arabia. King Hussein ended up in exile in Jordan where his son, Abdullah was made king not long before.

Syria was the first Arab country to gain independence and form a democratic government in 1949. But it also led the Arab world in military coups d'etat, starting with three in 1949 alone and followed by countless others. Under the Ottoman Empire prior to World War I, the Levant was known as Greater Syria and included Syria, Lebanon, and Palestine. Having defeated the Ottomans, the British and French divided the area so that the British maintained control of South Arabia and the eastern side of the Arabian Peninsula along the Gulf up to Iraq and won a mandate from the United Nations to govern Palestine and Transjordan. This was unfortunate, as the British had issued the Belfour Declaration in 1917 to create a homeland for Jews in Palestine, and the mandate gave them the opportunity to make it happen, at the expense of Palestinians.

The French got the rest of Greater Syria and split off Lebanon from Syria. They wrote a constitution for Lebanon based on sectarian politics; the President had to be a Maronite Christian, the Prime Minister had to be a Sunni Muslim, and the President of Parliament had to be a Shiiat Muslim. While it seemed to work in the 1950s, it carried the insidious seeds of division, culminating in a civil war twenty years later.

Arab countries in North Africa, other than Egypt and the Sudan, had little contact with the Levant and the Arabian Peninsula except for pilgrims traveling to Hejaz. A good number of these pilgrims settled in Hejaz over hundreds of years. We recognize many of them today by family names like Tunsi, Jazaeri, Maghrabi, or Shangeeti. Morocco was still a protectorate of France and its Sultan, Mohammad IV, was in exile in Madagascar for supporting an independence movement.

Algeria had been declared as an integral part of France with oppressive measures to eradicate the Arabic language and culture and encourage French ways in all aspects of life. A good number of French settlers, called Pieds Noir, had been there for years, but a bitter war of independence was raging. I remember an Egyptian film that was made based on the true story of an Algerian heroine of independence named Jamila Bu Haired, who captured the hearts of Arabs everywhere. Because of this and other more pressing societal upheavals, Charles de Gaulle, the President of France at the time, eventually granted independence to Algeria in 1961. Places like Tunis were not so lucky; the country was still a protectorate of France with a nominal head of state called the Bey or King. King Moncef called for independence unsuccessfully, and the leader of the national movement fighting for independence, Lahbib Bourguiba was held in prison by the French. France finally gave Tunis its independence on March 20, 1956 and Bourguiba became the first president, after abolishing the monarchy. We followed the news of these struggles in the Egyptian media, which led the Arab world then in both printed and audio-visual media.

Libya was a fledgling kingdom that gained its independence in 1951. It had been a colony of Italy from 1911 until 1943, when the allies took it from the Italians. The southwestern quadrant was administered by the French and the rest was administered by the British until 1951, when the United Nations declared Libya independent, and King Idris was installed as the first king.

This was the Arab World I read about in *Almosawar*, a world beginning to rise after centuries of subjugation with hope in a great future. It was a perfect time for Gamal Abdulnasser's call for Pan-Arab Nationalism to resonate with crowds all over the Arab World. Unfortunately, the resulting combination of military rule and naïve socialism that were promoted by Gamal Abdulnasser resulted in pain and chaos in many Arab countries over the next 70 years.

Contrasting today's Arab World with that of the 1950s, we easily conclude that countries where Gamal Abdulnasser's influence resulted in coups d'état and subsequent military rule have fared relatively badly in economic development and stability of government. These include Egypt, Iraq, Syria, Yemen, Libya, Mauritania, the Sudan, and Algeria. On the other hand, Arabian Gulf countries such as Jordan and Morocco fared much better—albeit to varying degrees depending on their wealth of natural resources.

21.

THE HADHRAMAUT DIASPORA

From the early days of Islam many people from Hadhramaut traveled to the Hejaz, the western part of Saudi Arabia today, to perform pilgrimage to Makkah. Most returned to Hadhramaut, but some stayed and integrated with the people of Hejaz, with some building significant business empires that still exist today. One attribute of Hadhramis was honesty and integrity, which meant that most money exchangers employed Hadhramis, and they also occupied key positions in private businesses that called for integrity and reliability. Every business had a cashier or treasurer, and these were invariably Hadhramis.

As Muslim armies pushed westward to reach Spain during the seventh century A.D., in the days of the Umayyad dynasty, Hadhramis joined the effort and finally settled all over North Africa. There is a famous letter written by Caliph Omar to Omar Ibn Al Aas, then Governor of Egypt, instructing him to appoint no judge but a Hadhrami, as they were known for integrity and fear of Allah. There is a cemetery in Cairo that is known as the "Cemetery of Hadhrami Judges."

Many Hadhrami last names start with the letters "Ba," somewhat like Mac in Gaelic names or O' in Irish names. It means "One with," followed by an attribute. For example, one who had a distinctive shape of head could be called "Baraas," with *raas* meaning head in Arabic. It was also used to refer to a grandfather. Baabdullah is a famous family name which probably started with a family calling its grandfather Ba Abdullah.

There are several families today in North Africa with such names that easily identify them as descendants of Hadhrami immigrants over the past 1,400 years. Such is the case in Africa, India, and East Asia. Whether names started with "Ba" or not, they helped maintain the umbilical cord tying Hadhramis to their mother country over the years.

I have been a part of someone's deeply personal story of heritage, history, and family with regard to their name. Ahmed was a dear friend in Saudi Arabia whose family emigrated from Wadi Doan over 300 years ago. The family name was Banaja, and it became one of the prominent families in Jeddah, on the west coast of Saudi Arabia. When I came to know him and his family history, I thought after 300 years, the "Ba" was the only link he had left with Hadhramaut. One year I organized a trip to tour Yemen and Hadhramaut and invited Ahmed along. He was enthusiastic about discovering Hadhramaut, and after we arrived there, he surprised me by asking to visit a place called Alrasheed in Wadi Doan, the town where his family emigrated from.

Our trip took us to Sanaa, the capital of unified Yemen, then Aden, Al Mukalla, and finally to Tarim. Once settled in a nice heritage hotel outside Tarim, we rented a Toyota Land Cruiser and drove from wadi to wadi over rough terrain for about three hours to get to Alrasheed. We had met some Banaja people in Al Mukalla who told us of a man called Salim Banaja in Alrasheed, who was a self-appointed historian of the family. After asking around, they told us he owned a shop that supplied the little town with food stuffs and household items.

They led us there and we found a young man who surprised us by saying that his father was expecting us; out came a short, wiry man with piercing eyes and a beautiful smile. My friend stepped up to introduce himself to the old man, saying, "I am Ahmad Sulaiman Banaja from Jeddah." And the old man replied, "You are Ahmed Sulaiman Abdulkader Karama Banaja." A person's full name traditionally starts with his given name, followed by his father's, his grandfather's, and so on for as long as a person wants or remembers. So, here is a man in the little town of Alrasheed in Wadi Hadhramaut who knows the lineage of my friend, whose family had left the wadi over 300 years earlier. The invisible tie that connects his family had never once broken—it had simply gotten longer.

The old man then insisted that we were his guests for three days, according to Hadhrami tradition, starting with a full lunch. We negotiated him down to three hours, which turned out to be one of the most enjoyable highlights of the trip to Yemen. Of course, the first thing we wanted to know was how he came to expect us. He said that the Banaja people in Al Mukalla sent him a message. He recited some of his poetry and spoke about the history of the Banaja clan who had emigrated over the years to many places including Egypt and East Africa.

At the end of our visit Old Man Salim took us to visit

the tomb of the father of the clan, who came to the wadi from Madinah, now in Saudi Arabia, over 1,200 years earlier; it was housed in a small mosque that was built by the ancestor himself. His family traces its lineage to the First Caliph Abubakr Al Siddiq and is one of many that has a deep and influential history with immigration.

22.

THE PERSONAL DIASPORA

People follow opportunity, for their betterment and that of their families. When men left Tarim and other parts of Hadhramaut in search of stability elsewhere, they left their wives and children behind in the care of a father, uncle, or brother and supported them with money earned in the diaspora. It became a tradition for a married woman to stay with her husband's family when her husband traveled for months and sometimes years. Given the hardships of travel by land and sea and the strict separation between the sexes, staying home was considered a way to maintain the dignity of women and spare them the hardships of travel. Not that they had any say in the matter; travel was hard, especially in the early nineteenth century. People rode camels for days to reach the coast before boarding sailing ships that traveled for weeks in dangerous waters to reach Africa, India, or the Far East, subject to the whims of the wind.

My father had hosted many people during their travels through Al Mukalla, so I enjoyed my time in the guesthouse with diaspora visitors. Some of them were born and raised in Indonesia or Singapore and learned Arabic as a second language. They had a strong accent, and most of them spoke broken Arabic. With Bahasa Melayu as their first language, they had a hard time attuning to the complexity of Arabic. Bahasa Melayu does not have verb conjugation nor gendered language, so they would sometimes address males as females or confuse tenses in Arabic, which amused me greatly. As I grew older, I had many questions to ask about the East and envisioned myself sitting on green mountains in Indonesia as described by the guests.

They always brought gifts that Father would bring home. I especially liked *kruppu* and *belanju* chips, which Mother would fry in hot oil. They would expand as they filled with air and were eaten as crunchy snacks or as garnish with meals. They also brought ginger preserve that had whole ginger roots in them, releasing its tangy, spicy, and sweet flavors ripened in syrup. Gifts also included batik cloth and velvet-covered black Indonesian head caps.

One of the visitors brought his thirteen-year-old daughter and ten-year-old son from Indonesia to his hometown, and father decided to invite them over to stay with Mother. They did not know a word of Arabic, but the girl said her name was Kodara. Mother had never heard that name before, and Father later explained that it was in fact Khadra, a rare name for a Hadhrami girl. It literally meant "green," but Hadhramis used it as an adjective for dark complexion. It made Khadra synonymous with Samra, a common female name in our language in parts of the Arab World, also of the same meaning.

There was also a dear friend of Father from Tarim who brought his eleven-year-old son to Al Mukalla to have him circumcised. The custom in Tarim was to circumcise boys between the ages of ten and twelve; by contrast, the people of Al Mukalla circumcised boys in their first week after birth and got it over with. The job was normally done by a barber using traditional methods and the whole thing was made into a celebration. The boy would be showered with gifts and a feast would be held for extended family members. Father's friend wanted his son to be circumcised by a doctor, as he considered the barber's way unsanitary, and Tarim did not have a doctor at that time. The operation was done in the hospital across the street in Al Mukalla, and the boy stayed in our home for a week. My father hosted many interesting visitors in the years our family was in Al Mukalla.

There is a saying in Hadhramaut: "In the money and not in the self." This is said to a person who loses something or has something broken, but themselves are relatively unharmed. It means that you are more important than the thing you lost, and that you will hopefully be able to replace it. When said in Arabic, it rhymes: "Fil mal wala fil hal." One visitor to Father's guesthouse was a distant relative who was well to do, being the beneficiary of a Singaporean family fund, but he was known to be tight-fisted. He was accompanied by a friend who was famous for being funny and witty. Our relative bought two delicate glass cylinders that were parts for a kerosene lamp (called Tilly Stormlight in Britain) to take to Tarim. As he was going upstairs holding a glass cylinder upright in each hand, he slipped and fell; but he made sure to fall on his elbows, thus saving the cylinders. His friend behind him shouted, "Fil hal Wala fil mal,' jokingly reversing the saying, meaning it was okay to get hurt, but save the goods.

Father's connection with the East started early in the nine-teenth century when his grandfather emigrated to Singa-pore. As was common practice, he was hosted by other, more settled Hadhramis. They lent him yards of different textiles to carry and sell door to door, and in time, he earned enough money to open a shop while learning Bahasa Me-layu along the way—though not fluently, as he could never learn to pronounce the letter "p," which does not exist in Arabic. Like other Hadhramis, he substituted the letter "f," which luckily did not exist in Bahasa Melayu to cause con-fusion. My great-grandfather's trade grew and expanded to Indonesia. He married three wives, with whom he fathered nine sons and two daughters. But he wanted to retire in his beloved Tarim, so he left his large family in Singapore. He married another woman in Tarim and fathered two more sons. The youngest of the two sons was born a few months after he died and was given the same first name as his father, according to custom.

People from different geographic areas in Hadhramaut tended to emigrate to their customary destinations. When early travelers from a certain area of Hadhramaut settled in a country or area and established themselves, others from their region or town were encouraged to follow them and received assistance from the earlier settlers. This is how trav-elers from certain areas in Hadhramaut ended up congregat-ing in certain areas.

Those from northern towns like Tarim and Seiyun gen-erally traveled to Singapore, Malaya, and Indonesia. People from the coastal areas generally immigrated to India and East Africa. Most from Wadi Doan in the center of Hadhramaut immigrated to India and East Africa, while some drifted northwest to Hejaz, now the western part of Saudi Arabia. There were exceptions, of course. For example, a group of my own clan went from Tarim to the Comoros Islands in Africa in the nineteenth century and became rulers from time to time. They also ruled a major Indonesian island called Aceh sometime in the nineteeenth century. The bulk of emigration was to the East, the Far East, and the eastern coast of Africa, where Hadhramis could travel by ship. There was little emigration to Europe and the Western Hemisphere, as no travel by sea was possible, especially before the Suez Canal was completed.

The tradition of movement, both temporary and permanent, is ingrained into our culture. And it didn't end with my father. The desire to move, to adapt, and to blend with new culture and terrains is deeply imbedded in each and every one of us.

23.

VISITING TARIM

A few weeks after my ninth birthday in 1956, Father announced that he was taking me along to Tarim for one month to attend the marriage of my older sister, the daughter of his second wife. I was excited to take my first plane trip and finally see Tarim and its people—to see the world beyond Al Mukalla. That day we drove out of the Al Mukalla gate and turned right toward Al Dees, then made another turn right and drove by Husn Al Ghowaizi (Al Ghowaizi Fort) that sat high on a hill on the left side of the dirt road. We had basically gone around the mountain and were driving behind Al Mukalla. Thirty minutes later, we entered the airport grounds and were greeted by Abdulghafour, the airport director. He looked more English than Indian, with his light complexion and his khaki shorts and short-sleeved shirt. He took us to his office and offered me an apple— a big treat, as apple and citrus trees did not grow in South Arabia's subtropical climate. At the time, apples and oranges were brought as gifts by pilgrims and other travelers, distributed to homes of relatives in one or two pieces. A family may gather around a single orange and eagerly watch the mother peel it before handing each one a segment to eat and savor slowly. In the moment, that apple was the most delicious thing I had ever tasted.

When it was time to take off, we walked a short distance to the DC-3 that was waiting for us and other passengers on the tarmac. In no time, I was strapped to a seat next to my father and waited excitedly for the plane to take off, a strange smell that I would associate with airplanes from then on permeating the air. The flight takes an hour to Al Ghuraf Airport outside Seiyun, less than 300 kilometers to the north, but it seemed an eternity toward the end. The view from the airplane window was captivating as we flew over mountain ranges; but the turbulence was fierce. Father grabbed the air sickness bag and opened it just in time for me to empty my stomach into it. I simply could not stop as the plane kept rocking my insides, and relief only came when the plane landed on a hard, compacted-dirt runway and taxied to the small airport building. Still, it was much better than traveling by caravan or automobile.

I saw my older brother, Abdullah, waiting with some relatives who traveled the 35 kilometers from Tarim to receive us. One of them took charge of delivering our luggage through security and paid customs on taxable goods since they arrived from outside the Kathiri Sultanate, but there was no passport control. They all kissed Father's right hand, led us to a waiting Land Rover, and started driving. Travelers had to pay customs again not 25 kilometers later, this time to the Qu'aiti Sultanate, because their borders were intertwined, which led to such ludicrous situations as double taxation.

Ten kilometers later we were in Tarim, and our first stop was the cemetery that housed the dead of the Baalawi tribe, which traced its lineage to the Prophet Mohammad. It was the first stop for any returning Baalawi sons. All graves were marked with brown tombstones made of clay that identified the one or more persons interred. The group took off their shoes at the entrance of the cemetery and headed to the center, where Al Fagih Al Mogaddam, the most venerable ancestor of all Baalawi, was buried. This area was covered with canvas and mats for people who wanted to spend time praying and meditating by the tomb. The group lined up and said a long prayer to Allah for the mercy and forgiveness of Al Fagih and all his descendants.

We walked solemnly out of the cemetery and drove to Father's home, where his uncle and his Tarim family waited for him. It was Father's turn to kiss his uncle's hand then embrace him before introducing me as I stood in awe of the old man, not knowing what to do or say. The old man smiled at me and extended his right hand for me to kiss, and I planted a loud kiss on it. This solicited some laughs, as kissing hands in Tarim is a silent action. In fact, they called the action "Shamma," meaning to smell.

For a while I sat politely next to my 23-year-old brother while Father and his uncle exchanged news and pleasantries. Then it was time to go meet the ladies in the other side of the house; Father's wife was obviously eager to see the son of the other wife. She smiled, kissed me, and asked me to call her Khala, meaning mother's sister. My fifteen-year-old sister was clearly happy to meet her new brother, and there was also my brother's wife, who happened to be the daughter of our aunt. Finally, there was my baby brother, Alawi, who was just beginning to take his first steps.

The next day was the start of a whirlwind of visits to family and friends and many lunches and dinners held in honor of Father. The first visit was in the afternoon to my only aunt and her husband, whom I called Amma (Father's sister). Amma was older than father, so it was Father's duty to kiss her hand. She had become the matriarch of a good sized family of four daughters (all married) and two sons, one of whom was Salem; I was glad to see him after two years.

The whole family had gathered to welcome Father and me. They were curious about me, a light complexioned newcomer who spoke in Al Mukalla dialect. During this attention-heavy meeting I was introduced to the son of one of my lady cousins, and we took to each other and would spend much time together during the month of the visit.

We were finally led to the main reception room to sit with the men of the house. A mat was laid with many delicacies including *kwailabees* (the Indonesian word for layer cake), canned cherries and pineapple, dates, figs, hot pancakes, and biscuits, among other desserts. Then to our delight, Bukhari tea was served. Tarim was famous for its Bukhari tea, which was named after Bukhara in Samarkand, Uzebekistan. Every sitting room had an area reserved for tea making with a samovar or bukhari, which was a stainless-steel or brass device with a tube in the middle filled with charcoal embers. Water boiled around the tube and was poured from a spout; then, a small porcelain pot was filled with tea leaves and boiling water and placed on top of the tube to keep hot. A bukhari would have a spout to pour boiling water from, while a samovar would use a faucet and was larger than a bukhari. Some of the strong tea in the small pot was poured in a small glass teacup to a fifth or half of the glass, depending on how strong the guest wanted his tea, then topped with hot water. A half to two cubes of sugar was usually added to taste.

Cousin Salem brought a large glass bottle with a strange top that had a spout and what looked like a trigger. He filled it with homemade lemonade, then placed a white pellet into the top and squeezed the trigger. The lemonade became fizzy and was served in small glasses. My only prior experience with a fizzy drink was in Al Mukalla when I followed my cousin Mohammad and his group to a park and he bought me Namnait, a local kind of lemonade. I remember watching wide-eyed as the bottle cap was popped and the drink inside fizzed. I had never tasted a fizzy drink that made my tongue tingle—a feeling never to be forgotten.

Soon after, as the evening was winding down, Salem showed me an adult size bicycle and asked me to try it. It was a challenge, as I had to reach down to the ground with the tip of my left toe to keep the bicycle upright when still. Cousin Salem said the bicycle was mine to use in Tarim for the duration of our stay there. I was ecstatic! But as my new friends did not have bicycles, I rarely used it.

The following days brought many visits to family and friends of Father, with similar mats of goodies but no fizzy drinks. Some residents of our area came to welcome Father, and I was shocked when an older man grabbed my hand to kiss it. I tried to withdraw my hand, but it was held firmly until it was kissed. After all, I was a descendant of the Prophet, and the old man was entitled to the blessing that came from kissing my hand. It took a while for the shock to wear off, since I was not used to this in Al Mukalla, where such customs were not strictly followed.

Eventually, people returned to their lives before we arrived, and my days in Tarim were filled with playing with my two Tarim friends and joining my father on some of his visits.

Father's uncle had two children, a son two years older than me and a daughter of around twelve. Ahmad and I did not click, as he was somewhat aggressive. One day, we were playing in the main reception room when he decided to wrestle me. I ran out and locked the door from the outside and just left him shouting for someone to release him. It took about an hour for someone to open the door, and thus ended a rather short-lived friendship. But I did play with two other boys, one of whom was the son of one of my lady cousins. We had a knack for inventing silly, simple, and physically exhausting games to fill our days. Not long after we arrived, I invented a game of athleticism and skill: we would run into the small mosque adjoining our home and deftly jump out of one its windows before repeating it all over again. I happened to be wearing a sarong one day instead of my usual shorts and decided to jump out of a window with a wooden pole sticking up from the ground outside. When my sarong became entangled in the pole, I ended up hanging upside down and unable to free myself until the two other boys saved me. I was embarrassed, but mostly unharmed. This is a memory I still held 50 years later, when I took my brothers and our male children on a trip to Tarim and the wooden pole was still there.

24.

THE WEDDING

My sister, Zainab, was betrothed to a distant cousin of the same family name. An indirect approach was made to our family to gauge its agreement before a direct approach was made to Father. In this case, the approach was to Father's uncle as the patriarch, in the absence of the father. The patriarch approved of the young man and wrote to Father, who readily agreed. Tradition dictated that girls had no say in the matter and would, ostensibly, not know until the day of the wedding, although this went against the dictate of Islam that mandated express agreement. The rationale was that fathers knew best, and that girls gave authority to their guardian to make the decision on their behalf.

Once the match was approved, a wedding date would be agreed upon, and the women of the family would gather on the appointed day at the girl's home with some excuse. The most senior relative would suddenly throw a large sheet over the girl and the rest of the women would break into *ha-*

jeer (the action of making loud sounds while wagging your tongue), also called *zaghrouta* in Egypt and Western Saudi Arabia. This would signal the start of the five-day wedding celebration, and a female band would immediately show up to start beating their tars and singing traditional wedding songs. The girl would often start crying out of shock and the sudden knowledge that she is leaving her family and the safety of her home. Of course, most girls already knew and cried because they were expected to.

The marriage customs of affluent families in Tarim were very elaborate. Weddings in families of lesser income were much more modest and may last only a day or two, and Al Mukalla marriage customs were also different and less extravagant.

This first step in Tarim is called Al Hakaa, which literal-ly meant "The Telling." A senior relative is charged with tell-ing the bride that she is getting married and the name of her groom. She continues to educate the girl in what marriage is and what happens between husband and wife.

In the days leading to my sister's wedding, I noticed excitement growing around the house with the approaching wedding date. On the appointed day, it was my aunt who threw the sheet over her, keeping her face covered the whole time, and was the first to hold her as she started to weep. The rest of the women then sat her on a decorated mattress in the middle of the room and went to work painting elaborate patterns on her hands and feet with henna while the female band appeared and started singing. The evening ended with dinner for the women of the extended family.

On the same evening, the groom was celebrated with Al Mariah at his family home, where the elders of his extended

family and selected invitees would gather after the last evening prayer. I accompanied my father and brother as guests
to the Mariah and sat fascinated by all the action. The evening started with dinner after which the Ba Saleh band started beating their *marawees* (small hand-held drums) and *daffs*
(tambourines). The rhythm was called *zerbadi* and the songs
they sang were Bani Meghrah lyrics. Men of all ages rose to
dance to the zerbadi beats. This was an evening for the elders
to let loose and dance in celebration of the wedding of their
young man. The climax of the evening was applying henna
to the feet of the groom; a decorated mattress was laid in the
middle and the groom sat while two men would mix henna
and water and apply it. Everyone went around them dancing and singing a special song for this occasion.

Thus went the first evening, with separate celebrations
at the homes of the bride and groom.

On the second day, the house of the bride came alive
soon after the dawn prayers, with men showing up to
slaughter ten lambs, some of which had been gifted by relatives. Once slaughtered, the lambs would be hanged by their
hind legs, skinned, and cut in a specific way to minimize
waste. Even the trotters (various body parts, including the
feet) are saved for later use. The men who slaughtered and
prepared the meat and the men who cooked the food were
all men of the community who did not claim any pay for
their service except being part of the festivities. Every quarter of Tarim had a Mogaddam (the Chief, translated to "the
advanced one") who organized participation in weddings,
funerals, and public festivities, and also served as arbiter to
settle disputes. This system was created and has survived as a
form of local municipal government for hundreds of years.

Although I went to bed late the night after returning from Al Mariah, I woke up early looking forward to the events of the day. I rushed downstairs to see the men at work, luckily after the lambs were slaughtered and hanged. I spent the day watching the preparation of the food and running upstairs to see the ladies preparing the bride. I was fascinated by the transformation of my teenage sister into a made-up, beautiful bride wearing a richly designed wedding dress and adorned with gold on her hands, arms, and around her neck. She had what looked like a round and wide black turban on her head decorated with gold and jewelry. I was told that it was called *esabah*, which is an expensive heirloom kept in the family and used in family weddings for generations. This particular Esabah was apparently famous around Tarim and belonged to my aunt.

The relatives of the groom gathered in his home after the mid-afternoon prayer then walked to our home led by a Khedam Al Saggaf band that beat small round drums and played flutes as they sang incomprehensible songs. Following the band were the elders of the groom's clan surrounding the groom, and the religious leader who was to officiate the wedding, then the rest of the groom's family men. Walking beside the groom was an older gentleman holding a 200-year-old hand-held fan made of palm leaves; he was called Al Ata. His job was to ensure the groom's good appearance and fan him as necessary. He also told the groom what to do and where to sit. This occupation was inherited from father to son along with the fan. This procession was called Al Harawa. They were received outside the bride's home by Father, his son, his uncle, and close relatives, who led the guests to the upper floor reception room where other guests were already waiting. The wedding was usually offici-ated by a religious leader, and in our case, it was the Mufti of Tarim. A town's mufti is the highest authority in inter-preting the Quran and Sunnah, a consultant to individuals and the government who was invited from time to time by prominent families to officiate their weddings.

The officiator sat in the center of the large room with Fa-ther and the groom sitting in front of him (Al Ata stood next to the groom and fanned the three). The ceremony start-ed with the officiator or his assistant reciting the marriage speech, which was a standard confirmation of the sanctity of marriage and the duties of bride and groom, and ended with a prayer for Allah to bless the two with good children. He asked Father and the groom to hold each other's right hand as in a handshake, then asked Father to address the groom by his name and state that he gave him his daughter (stating her name) in marriage according to the laws of Allah and his prophet's sunnah at a dowry of three silver leaves of Tarim standard. The dowry is given by the groom to the bride and called "Mahr." The amount is supposed to be declared pub-licly and in the wedding document, but Tarim families use this standard phrase as they do not wish to declare the exact amount agreed between the two families. The reason is that it could be a juicy piece of gossip if some thought it to be too small or too large. It could also be a matter of compe-tition among families as to who paid or received the higher amount.

The officiator then asked the groom to repeat after him, "I accept her marriage." The process is repeated three times for confirmation. Then the officiator would pray to Allah to bless the bride and groom and grant them good offspring before informing all present that they were witnesses to the marriage. Young men circulated immediately after with plates of roasted sesame seeds for guests to scoop with their fingers and eat the seeds out of their palms. (I noticed some of the men grabbing big handfuls to stuff into their pockets.)

Al Harawa dinner was then served before sunset. A number of round palm leaf carpets called *tefals* were brought in, and men automatically formed circles of five to six around each tefal. Round large plates of fried rice would be placed in the middle with several small dishes of spicy *sambal* surrounding the rice plate, then two men circulated with one holding a large plate full of cooked meat on his head. The other grabbed pieces of meat and placed them in front of each guest. The elders received large, juicy pieces, then portions got smaller and less meaty as the plates got farther away from the elders. Everyone then dug in, using their bare right hands. After the meal, young men would bring water and soap for the elders to wash their hands in large bowls while others walked out to wash their greasy hands outside. Bukhari tea was then served to complete the meal, and the men left.

The groom stayed behind with his close relatives while my sister was being prepared to be seen by her husband for the first time after he gained the legal right to see her, her mother, and grandmother earlier in the afternoon. Father, my older brother, and I walked the groom to the room where the three of them sat. The *Cobara* (lady specializing in hair dressing and make up of brides) was hovering over the bride to make sure her clothes and hair were perfect; my sister's mother welcomed the groom and invited him to sit next to his bride, who averted her eyes in shyness. He awkwardly mumbled a few nice words and took out a large gold necklace and draped it around my sister's neck with shaking hands. Tea was served and the groom left after a half hour of chit-chat.

Later in the evening, the groom returned with a few close relatives to take his bride to her new home. The female band beat their drums and sang my sister to the door of her home along with her mother and some close women relatives. My older brother and I joined the procession as my sister left the house and walked with her husband to his home, where she was received by the high voices of the family women, rising with hajeer. My sister's mother stayed with her until the groom came in to make sure that she was comfortable and helped her arrange her clothes and looks. By now, the groom had become a *Mahram* to the bride's mother, meaning that he was like a son to her, and she did not have to veil her face or cover her hair in his presence.

The Sobha ("the morning after") was held on the third day, when the groom's family invited all the male relatives of the bride to an early lunch that was served between 10:00 and 11:00. This was a home cooked meal with a good number of delicious dishes. By noon, all male guests except close relatives who were able to see the bride had left. We were led to her room where my sister and her husband sat. We sat with them for around twenty minutes, making small talk and giving the bride *takhaweed* (wedding gifts) before going home. Then it was the turn of the female relatives of the bride to be served a big meal in the middle of the afternoon. This was called Al Thalla lunch followed by party time with female singers beating drums and leading the bride from her room to the gathering. Women rose to dance two at a time, and the party went well into the evening.

The fourth day celebration was called Al Saffa, during which close relatives of both bride and groom were invited to the groom's family home for a mid-day lunch. Lunch was followed with tea, and the men soon left. The number of women grew and a good number of well-wishers from outside the family circle went to celebrate, the party continuing until sunset.

The fifth and final event in the wedding celebrations was Al Khatra ("the step"), because it was the first step that the bride takes outside her new home, and it must be to her family's home. The bride's family celebrated the return of their daughter along with her groom on her first visit and invited her close relatives to lunch along with close relatives of her groom. Once again, the men came for the food then left, but the women stayed on and partied into the evening with singing and dancing.

I missed Zainab after she moved to her husband's home. I used to ask Khala to give me something to take to Zainab because I felt I needed an excuse to go visit her. I had missed the times we spent together before she got married. She would be ready with roasted seeds of a vegetable of the pumpkin family, having spent considerable time extracting the inside of the seeds for me. She obviously missed me, too.

A day before departing back to Al Mukalla, news arrived of the death of Sultan Saleh. I was not used to death as a natural event and had horrifying mental images of it. That night, I had a nightmare of the Sultan's funeral procession passing by my window in Al Mukalla, and I could see the dead body inside the box.

The next day, Father and I bade farewell to everyone. Unbeknown to anyone then, including Father, it would be Father's final goodbye. Several well-wishers accompanied us to the airport, along with my brother, Abdullah. The return trip was less painful this time, and I enjoyed the view from the airplane of the flat plateau with large and small wadis carved in it.

Mother was waiting with open arms and had many questions for me. She asked many questions but was circumspect in her questions about Khala.

I did not fall asleep quickly but lay in bed remembering all the experiences I had over the past month and thinking how life in Tarim was so different from Al Mukalla. Of course, Father's visit and the wedding raised much more excitement than daily life would normally entail in sleepy Tarim. Al Mukalla was different in many ways. There was the ocean and the port with all the hustle and bustle you find around port cities. It was also a capital city with all the goings on around the Sultan and the government. But mostly the difference was because of the mix of people of different backgrounds, religions, accents, and social customs.

It would be thirty-eight years before I saw Tarim again and met my youngest brother for the first time; he was born nine months after Father and I left Tarim.

25.

MOVING TO SAUDI ARABIA

Soon after returning to Al Mukalla, I learned that Dada and the rest of Mother's family were moving to Jeddah, Saudi Arabia to join Uncle Abdulrahman, who was now doing well in business in the land of opportunities. Less than a year earlier he had sent a sleek 1955 Ford sedan for his father and brothers to use; a beautiful red and white car with winged back lights, it was all the rage in American car models at the time. On the day of the trip Dada, Hababa, several grandchildren, one uncle, and three aunts were loaded into several cars (one being the sedan) with several pieces of luggage.

We drove along leveled dirt roads, with much dust raised by each car. Once the caravan of cars turned behind the mountain and was driving in a flat wadi, the driver of the Ford picked up speed and I had a view of the beautiful car sailing across the wadi with plumes of dust trailing it. That wonderful image never left my memory.

Mother was the only member of her family remaining behind in Al Mukalla, so the farewell at the airport was quite emotional. I was fascinated by all the activity around me, the terminals, and the few planes on the tarmac, so I did not follow the family conversation that would have told me of the impending move of my own family to Jeddah. Unbeknownst to me, this would kickstart the beginning of a new life that took me to every continent around the world with experiences beyond the imagination of a young, small-town boy.

It was the end of June and the school summer holiday had already started when I learned of our planned trip to Saudi Arabia. The family was ostensibly going for the Hajj, which was taking place around the middle of July that year. Mother was told to pack as little as possible, and Father told her we were coming back after Hajj and visiting her family. (In fact, neither of my parents returned, and it would be 37 years before I saw Al Mukalla again.) It was not clear then whether Father intended to return soon or if his plans were already set on staying in Saudi Arabia. But I have come to believe since that he did not intend to return in the short term. He simply did not wish to leave Al Mukalla with people thinking he ran away, so he instead announced that he was going to the Hajj.

However, having later learned of the collapse of the tobacco deal, which left him in a very weak business position, he was probably finding it difficult to pick up the pieces and bring his business back to health. As it happened, he gave his young assistant, Mohammad Bin Yahia, full authority to manage his affairs after his departure. Some prominent businessmen stepped in soon enough, helping the young man sell remaining assets, settle debts, and tie up other affairs before he was not a part of our lives any longer.

Mohammad Bin Yahia, known as simply Bin Yahia by almost everyone, was my father's trusted assistant in Al Mukalla. He was nice and kind and I never hesitated to ask him for coins to buy sweets. I had lost contact with him since departing Al Mukalla until decades later when I found him in Abu Dhabi. He had tried to adapt to life under the People's Democratic Republic of South Yemen but eventually ran away to the UAE, where he settled and built a comfortable life for himself and his family. With Father dying at a relatively young age, I was still ignorant of much of his life before we moved to Saudi Arabia. He rarely spoke about himself, and I was not old enough to be curious. So, finding Bin Yahia was a golden opportunity to learn about Father's business life in Al Mukalla.

I had always sensed a sadness in my father after leaving Al Mukalla but never questioned it when I was young. Bin Yahia started by telling me about how he came to work with Father. He was born in Singapore to a father who came from Tarim and a Singaporean-born mother. His father decided to bring his wife, three daughters, and young son to Tarim. But after two years, he decided to move with his family to the coast. Unfortunately, he died two weeks after the move, when Bin Yahia was only 14. I learned how Father took the family under his wing and asked Bin Yahia to come work with him. Bin Yahia took to Father's flourishing business easily and became a trusted and effective assistant within two years. These were the peak years of Father's professional life; his transport business was growing, and he'd gotten new contracts in supplying the Qu'aiti Sultanate government and army. Bin Yahia told me how he admired Father's entre-preneurial spirit and his courageous risk-taking.

Then Father became excited about an excellent business opportunity being promoted by a trusted friend. It involved satisfying Egyptian high demand for tobacco with good quality tobacco which was grown near the Hadhramaut coast. The idea was to contract farmers to grow a shipload of the tobacco then ship it to sell on the Cairo commodity bourse (exchange). This required considerable capital, and other Al Mukalla businessmen participated with significant amounts of cash. Father sank everything he had into the project, which proceeded well until the tobacco reached Cairo. As luck would have it, no sooner had it arrived in storage in January 1952 than the great Cairo fire broke out. The fire consumed a large area in the center of Cairo—in-cluding the tobacco shipment. Father lost all he had save some assets and a piece of land that housed his truck depot.

At the same time, his aging fleet of small two-and-a-half ton trucks, which had dominated the transportation scene in the 1940s, was steadily losing market to the much larg-er trucks that were being introduced by new competitors. Contracts for supplying the government and the army were infrequent and insufficient to meet general expenses. The business steadily got worse and worse and was floundering by the beginning of 1956. Uncle Abdulrahman apparently heard of the catastrophic event and stepped in with an offer for Father to come manage a tile factory he owned in Ri-yadh, and Father accepted.

And so, fate had it that tobacco would be the root cause for our move to Saudi Arabia at that time, and the great life I have experienced since.

We were at Al Rayyan Airport once again on the last day of June, waiting for our DC-3 to take off to Jeddah. I saw Father holding a red passport and another green one and asked to see them. The red one had my mother's name and those of her five children; in place of a photo of my mother the word "Veiled" was written. The green passport was Father's passport, complete with his photo. The red passport was issued by the Qu'aiti Sultanate and the green passport was issued by the Kathiri Sultanate, but both passport pages had water marks on every page that read "British Passport."

As we waited to board, I sat alone thinking of all the exciting experiences since the beginning of the year and wondering what my new world would be like.

26.

JEDDAH

Moving to Jeddah was a leap in time. Even heading out of the airport, I was in awe of the asphalted streets lined by modern buildings. Street intersections were governed by a traffic policeman standing in the middle and operating a manual signal device, a pole topped by a cross that the policeman rotated from time to time. The cross was painted green on two side and red on the other two sides, and he positioned the red sides facing the streets he wanted to stop traffic from and the green side facing the streets allowed to flow. Before any change, the policeman blew a whistle to warn drivers. The streets were busy with people, cars, bicycles, and donkeys pulling carts that carried goods, water, or kerosene, and lined by shops of all kinds including restaurants and cafes. I could smell falafel frying and chicken roasting.

We finally stopped at my uncle's house, a large two-story home that was milling with family members and guests from Hadhramaut who came for the pilgrimage that was to start in one week. There was much hugging, kissing, and crying before we settled down to hear about life in Jeddah from those who came two months earlier.

The move was a dizzying whirlwind, but the highlight of my first day in Jeddah was watching bottles of Kitty Cola popped open, the cola drink fizzing before each of us had a bottle to enjoy. I curiously watched as one of the girls collected all the bottle caps and started to remove the cork lining of the caps, looking for an alphabetic letter. It turns out that the Kitty Cola factory was printing one of the letters in Kitty Cola on the inside of the caps, promising a Japanese car to anyone collecting the full set spelling out "KITTY COLA."

I tagged along with the cook on the following day to a nearby shop the and saw a man buying a whole box of Kitty Cola bottles. He did not drink any but popped all the bottles and scraped the cork looking for letters on the inside of the caps. Kitty Cola sales were skyrocketing, but after two months of frenzied consumption, only two cars were won, as the company had printed the letter C only twice. Life was so different here than in Al Mukalla.

As I closed my eyes to sleep that night, I could only see bottles of fizzing liquid behind my eyelids, and I felt with absolute certainty that on that day, my life had changed forever.

We had arrived in Jeddah two days before the Hajj (pilgrimage), which Father had been eager to perform as a pillar of his faith. He left to Riyadh to take over the tile plant and we stayed in Jeddah for six months before Father returned to take us to Riyadh. But he brought us back to Jeddah every summer to visit our grandparents and the rest of the family.

Dada lived in much the same way that he lived in Al Mukalla, mostly staying at home with his Quran and his Urdu and Persian books of religion and poetry. The move to Jeddah fulfilled Dada's wish to be close to the holy city of Makkah, only 82 kilometers away, and his sons took him there as often as he wanted. He passed away seven years after leaving Hadhramaut and was taken to be buried in Makkah, which was his final wish. We children carried on with life in our adopted country, from which our ancestors had emigrated more than a thousand years earlier, blending with its people and growing up to be good citizens contributing to the country's development. But we never forgot our roots and the people we left behind in the old country next door.

27.
TIME PASSES

It had been 38 years since I had set eyes on Hadhramaut, and 27 years since Cousin Salem left. He had ended up in Riyadh in 1966 after some years spent in Aden working for a company in Riyadh for a few years before setting up his own business with a trusted friend, using their good command of English to represent several Japanese and Korean companies. Saleh and I were both established businessmen in 1993 and we had kept in touch all those years, so we decided to venture to see what happened to Hadhramaut—our homeland.

By now, Tarim had become a part of the Yemen Arab Republic in the province of Hadhramaut. The full merger of the Yemen Arab Republic and the People's Democratic Republic of South Yemen was consummated in 1990, soon after the collapse of the Soviet Union. People of the South were now free of travel restrictions and the socialist regime, though the aftershocks stayed for many years after.

We traveled first class on Yemen Airways and visited Sanaa for a few days before flying to Aden to tour the town and enjoy the hospitality of several relatives living there. When we landed in Tarim, we were met at Al Ghuraf Airport by my three brothers and Salem's nephews. We followed the same routine of stopping at the cemetery before separating and visiting our respective family homes. My brother Abdullah was now 59 years old and a grandfather. My brother Alawi, who was barely taking his first steps when I left him in 1956, was now a man of 39 with a wife and children. I saw my brother Hussain for the first time at the airport. He was now 36, also married with children. Time had flown by in an inevitable, yet almost imperceptible way. I never lost touch with my siblings in Hadhramaut. They needed economic support, which my brothers and I provided over the years. Of course, my older brother was the link, especially as he was able to travel and visit us in Saudi Arabia.

Not much changed in Hadramaut in 38 years. The dirt road from the airport was now an asphalt road; so was the main road in Tarim. Tarim was still a sleepy town enjoying a slow and peaceful rhythm of life. It was as if history had left Tarim behind on its march forward. I remembered a welcome sign at Sanaa airport early in the trip which read, "Welcome to Yemen, the Living Museum." It was truly an apt description.

Our plan was to stop and see Al Mukalla after one week in Tarim. We rented a Toyota Land Cruiser for the trip to add even more to the nostalgia, even though it wasn't necessary anymore. The road was now asphalted all the way to Al Mukalla, and the drive took around five hours along deep wadis that narrowed and expanded. Some were quite green while others were barren, depending on the amount of water that was retained after good rains. We finally had to cross a high mountain range and the road became steep and winding all the way to the top, the driver constantly shifting gears until we reached a rest stop.

We were quite hungry by then and ordered the only dish available, which was rice with lamb meat. Three of us sat around a good sized, steaming plate that smelled heavenly. I asked for a spoon to use, and suddenly all conversation around me stopped. I looked at the man serving the food who laughed and said they did not have any for eating, only the large ones to scoop with. I was expected to use the five fingers of my right hand like everyone else. That was the way I ate before leaving Hadhramaut, and that was the way people still did. I smiled and dug in gingerly with my hand.

We resumed our drive on the plain until the road took a steep and winding slide on the other side of the mountain range. From the bottom of the mountain to Al Mukalla was only around 40 kilometers, and it was not long until we reached the Hadhramaut Hotel on the beach in Khalf, resting there until the next day.

We decided to drive west from Khalf to the western end of the town and tried to recall the landmarks along the way; yet every time I thought we would surely get to one, the driver would say we'd already passed it. It seems distances in adulthood are much shorter than in childhood memories. The buildings were smaller, some places had been repurposed, and most empty spaces were built upon or destroyed. I discovered that Alrawdha Mosque no longer sat on the beach with waves lapping at its wall, as nearly one hundred meters were reclaimed from the sea to build a wide road behind it and a wide walk overlooking the rocky beach. Al Mukalla gate was gone because the first revolutionary mayor of Al Mukalla after independence considered it a bourgeois feature that had to be obliterated. Sharj was no longer a town of shacks but rather a nice suburb of Al Mukalla. Given the limited space in Fortress Al Mukalla, the town expanded westward with considerable growth toward Al Sharj and Addees. It also expanded to the east beyond Khalf, especially as the road from Khalf was widened towards the airport.

Slightly disoriented and hoping to find something I recognized, I asked the driver to return to the town to look for our old home. Luckily, I found it easily, almost unchanged. A third floor was added after we departed, but the structure remained the same. But what I looked forward to doing most in Al Mukalla was finding Sehala. Cousin Salem and I set out the following morning to look for her near our old home. We stopped at the old shop and the owner knew Sehala, pointing to the building where she lived. The two-story building was built where there used to be a single-story structure. But it was also built of stones and noora and looked no different than the house I grew up in. It was very dark inside as we entered the building and went upstairs to her apartment. The door was open, so I stuck my head in and called her name. She said to come in and I stepped in with my cousin Saleh behind me, the room still dark. I could barely see her in what looked like the kitchen, but I called my name out so she would know it was me. She brightened up, looked behind me, and said, "Of course, and you brought your cousin Salem with you." Incredible! She had seen neither of us for more than 37 years and could still recognize us both in the dim light.

We sat with her for two hours, conveyed Mother's greeting and warm wishes, and traveled down memory lane. She was on her own now. She had lived with her old husband, Mahfouz, and her older sister, Masaad, but they had both died in the last two years. She told us how hard her brother tried to bring her to live with him and his family in Sharj, but she resisted because she valued her independence.

I went back to Al Mukalla once again 10 years later with my brothers and our sons and went looking for Sehala in the same apartment. But we learned that her brother finally prevailed and took her to live with him. She was steadily losing her sight and had already caused a fire in her kitchen, so she had finally acquiesced to her brother and went to live with him until she passed. We found the place and went to see her. It was a great and emotional reunion of Sehala and the children she helped raise, who came to show her their children. She remembered every day of our lives with her and told all the funny episodes with each of us. She, of course, also complained about being away from her own home. She died not long after our visit.

We were invited to dinner at the home of Salem's nephew, who served grilled sardines. I could not have asked for anything better, and the first morsel I placed in my mouth brought a flood of memories. The sardines were in season and were fat and juicy, so that I would simply slide my finger across a sardine and its skin would peel off easily.

The next day, Cousin Salem and his son wanted to return to Aden, so they bade me farewell. Not long after, I was on the road to Al Rayyan Airport once again to fly back to Sanaa then onward to Riyadh. I watched as the sun glinted off the wadis and hills as they had 37 years ago, the airport buildings looming ahead. The only real difference, I thought, was the Boeing 737 jets (instead of the rickety DC-3 propeller aircraft) noisily ascending into the sky, flying people to faraway places.

EPILOGUE

It has been 66 years since I left Al Mukalla to Saudi Arabia. While the latter has developed and grown 10 times in population and many times in wealth and prosperity, Yemen and South Arabia have regressed to chaos and poverty. After 23 years of socialist rule, South Arabia, with less than four million people, merged with Yemen to the north with 20 million people in 1990. Tribal peace, orderly government, and the relatively high level of literacy of the south were married to the chaotic and corrupt government of the north, where nearly 40 million firearms were in the hands of tribes and individuals. The north was further plagued with a national addiction to *qat*, a plant leaf that was chewed and had a similar effect to amphetamines.

It does not take much intelligence to imagine the calamitous result of such a marriage. Within four years of the union, the south tried to break away in 1994, leading to a civil war that killed 10,000 people. The south lost and the result was full dominance by the north until the more recent war.

Yemen has been in the grip of a civil war that has raged for seven years, pitting a rebel group that swept down from the north, with the support of the Islamic Republic of Iran, and the legal government that went into exile for some time while the rebel group swept across the whole country. With the support of Saudi Arabia and the United Arab Emirates, the legal government of Yemen managed to build an army, free the south and its capital, Aden, and push the rebels back. But momentum stalled and fighting has gone on for years, resulting in many deaths and misery for all people in both regions.

In the 32 years since merging north and south, Hadhramaut stood as a cynical spectator, suffering the fallout from bad government but luckily avoiding much of the bloodshed. Its sons and daughters in the diaspora are extending lifelines to many families there in the meantime, waiting patiently and holding out hope for peace, sanity, and good government to return. They can then safely return, invest, and bring this place into the twenty-first century.

ACKNOWLEDGMENTS

Thank you to every person who has played a hand in culti-
vating my love of travel, education, and culture. I am grateful for all of my past and present tutors, religious leaders,
and friends, as well as my wonderful family, for making me
the person I am today. I am proud of my land's history and
potential and hope to inspire Hadhramis around the globe
to pursue a deeper connection with the Hadhramaut region
of South Arabia.

I would also like to extend a special thanks to Aisha,
Bill, Jennifer, Debbie, and Nayla, who helped me make this
book more readable.

AUTHOR BIOGRAPHY

Ahmad Al Sari was born in 1947 in Al Mukalla, Hadhramaut. His family decided to move to Saudi Arabia in 1956, where he lived out the rest of his childhood surrounded by rich culture and customs. His experiences and environment propelled his life forward and taught him the value of family, faith, and continuous learning.

After receiving primary and secondary education, Al Sari studied at King Fahd University of Petroleum & Minerals, then transferred to the University of Texas at Austin to earn a chemical engineering degree in 1970. He returned home to commence a career in computer programming (a nascent technology field at the time), at King Fahd University. He progressed to manage the university's computer center in 1976.

In 1979, Al Sari put his experience and visibility as technology pioneer to use and co-founded his first IT services business, helping it grow to a group of companies employing over 8,500 people across the Arabian Gulf. After years of success and technological evolution, he co-founded a technology investment firm in 2010 and is now a technology investor and author.

Al Sari is married with five adult children and seven grandchildren, and he hopes to use his history to help them find their roots in South Arabia and the Hadhramaut region.

For more information and further reference, Al Sari recommends *A Brief History of Hadhramaut* by Mohammad Abdulkader Bamatraf (Dar Hadhramaut for Studies & Publishing).

www.ingramcontent.com/pod-product-compliance
Lightning Source LLC
Chambersburg PA
CBHW031524120626
46545CB00005B/1989